DEVELOPMENTAL PSYCHOLOGY FOR THE HEALTH CARE PROFESSIONS

Part 1
Prenatal Through Adolescent Development

BEHAVIORAL SCIENCES
FOR HEALTH CARE PROFESSIONALS
Michael A. Counte, Series Editor

During the 1970s there was rapid growth in the amount of behavioral science instruction included in the training of physicians, nurses, dentists, pharmacists, and other health care professionals. New faculty members were put on staffs at medical centers, curricula were devised, and on occasion, new departments were created to support a diverse group of behavioral scientists.

The new emphasis on behavioral science in the education of health care professionals and the inclusion of a behavioral science section in certification examinations have generated a need for clinically relevant text materials. This series responds to that need by providing general, yet concise, introductions to common topical areas in behavioral science curricula, linking concepts and theories to clinical practice.

The authors of the series volumes are behavioral scientists with considerable experience in the education of health care professionals. Most of them are also clinicians, and their varied experience enables them to present their topics in a readable fashion. The content of the texts presumes only a very basic knowledge of the behavioral sciences, and emphasis is placed on the practical implications of research findings for health care delivery.

It is our hope that this multivolume approach will allow each instructor to select the books most pertinent to his or her particular curriculum. The division of topics was planned to enhance the overall flexibility of the information being presented.

Titles in This Series

Also of Interest

† Available in hardcover and paperback.

DEVELOPMENTAL PSYCHOLOGY FOR THE HEALTH CARE PROFESSIONS: PART 1 – PRENATAL THROUGH ADOLESCENT DEVELOPMENT

Katherine A. Billingham, Ph.D.

Rush University
Rush–Presbyterian–St. Luke's Medical Center

In this book, the first of a two-volume set focusing on normal psychological development throughout the life span, Katherine A. Billingham discusses the basics of normal development and presents specific research findings in developmental psychology, sociology, and health care psychology that are especially relevant to the health care professional.

Beginning with an overview of developmental concepts, methodological issues, and the work of three major developmental theorists – Freud, Piaget, and Erikson – Dr. Billingham goes on to explain the developmental process from prenatal and infancy stages through adolescence. For each age group, physical, cognitive, sexual, and personality development are discussed, as well as the role of the family and special health care considerations.

With this information, health care professionals should be better able to relate their patients' physical, social, and psychological functioning to appropriate age and sex norms; to evaluate the nature and causes of deviations and take proper steps for further evaluation, referral, or treatment; and to understand how health and illness can influence or modify individual development.

Dr. Katherine A. Billingham is assistant professor in the Department of Psychology and Social Science, Rush University, and assistant scientist on the medical staff at Rush–Presbyterian–St. Luke's Medical Center in Chicago.

BEHAVIORAL SCIENCES FOR HEALTH CARE PROFESSIONALS

DEVELOPMENTAL PSYCHOLOGY FOR THE HEALTH CARE PROFESSIONS

Part 1 – Prenatal Through
Adolescent Development

Katherine A. Billingham, Ph.D.

Rush University,
Rush-Presbyterian-St. Luke's Medical Center

Westview Press / Boulder, Colorado

Behavioral Sciences for Health Care Professionals

Copyright © 1982 by Westview Press, Inc.

Published in 1982 in the United States of America by
Westview Press, Inc.
5500 Central Avenue
Boulder, Colorado 80301
Frederick A. Praeger, Publisher

Library of Congress Cataloging in Publication Data
Billingham, Katherine A.
   Developmental psychology for the health care professions.
   (Behavioral sciences for health care professionals)
   Includes bibliographical references and index.
   Contents: pt. 1. Prenatal through adolescent development.
   1. Developmental psychology. I. Title. II. Series.
BF713.B54   155'.02461   81-16012
ISBN 0-86531-000-9 (v. 1)   AACR2
ISBN 0-86531-001-7 (pbk.: v. 1)

Printed and bound in the United States of America

BE
5-13-82

In Memory of E. K. Billingham, R.N., M.A.

CONTENTS

CONTENTS

TABLES AND FIGURES

DEVELOPMENTAL PSYCHOLOGY FOR THE HEALTH CARE PROFESSIONS

Part 1
Prenatal Through Adolescent Development

STAGES OF HUMAN DEVELOPMENT: AN OVERVIEW

THE LIFE-SPAN VIEWPOINT

The goal of the study of human development is to obtain a complete picture of the sequence of age-related changes that occur within a lifetime. Because all aspects of human development are interrelated and integrated, each change must be understood within the context of (1) past experience; (2) other developing compentencies; and (3) the individual's social network. This understanding is necessary for health professionals to function as educators in the prevention of disease, facilitators of family support, and caretakers of the physically ill.

Influences of Past Experiences

The description of life-span development used in this volume will be age-organized in order to highlight the logical sequence of time. Within this context, it will become clear that mastering the tasks of one period forms the basis for mastering the tasks of the next developmental era. Each phase of development has characteristic traits, a period of equilibrium when the individual adjusts more easily to intrinsic and environmental demands, and a period of disequilibrium when adjustment is more difficult (Erikson 1963; Mussen, Conger, and Kagan 1974; and Sullivan 1953). If the developmental tasks are not accomplished or their accomplishment is delayed, the individual will have difficulties in later stages. For example, if a pregnant woman suffers severe malnourishment, the child she is carrying may not develop the normal number of brain cells and may therefore be born mentally defective. Also, infants who spend their first months in very dull, unstimulating environments appear to be deficient in cognitive skills and perform poorly on tests of intellectual ability when older. Conversely, the successful completion of a developmental task at one age becomes the foundation for later accomplishments. The child who develops a basic understanding of cause-and-effect relationships is capable of thinking abstractly later on.

Influences of Other Developing Competencies

For the purposes of discussion it will be necessary to isolate specific aspects of development such as physical growth, cognitive development, or identity formation. This gives a somewhat inaccurate picture of the developmental process, because development in one function is likely to affect development in another. For example, while a child is maturing physically (probably, in large measure, as a result of genetic factors), intellectual capabilities are expanding, abilities to reason and think logically are improving. At the same time, the child's personality and social behavior are being modified, partly as a result of these physical and cognitive developments and partly as a result of social experiences. In turn, changes in personality and social behavior will be having an effect on intelligence and cognitive abilities. Thus it is important to remember that aspects of development interact with and influence one another at all stages.

In this volume, development in five main areas will be discussed for each age group. The areas are: physical, cognitive, identity, sexual, and social development. Physical competencies include various motor and neurological capabilities to attain mobility, manipulation, and care for oneself physically. Cognitive competencies include learning how to perceive, think, and communicate thoughts and feelings. Identity formation includes developing an awareness and acceptance of oneself as a separate person and coping with internal and external stresses within a social network. Sexual development includes the acceptance of physical changes due to either growth or illness, the development of a positive body image, and the creation of intimate relationships. Finally, social competence includes learning how to securely affiliate with the family and particiate with a wider social network.

Influences of the Social Network—The Family

The third context in which developmental change must be viewed is that of the individual's social network. The primary social network is the family, which influences an individual's development in two major ways: First, the family regulates the information brought into the family. It teaches and nurtures; it sets goals, ideals, and values for its members. Second, the family consists of members, each of whom is at a different stage of development. These differences influence each individual's perspective on their own personal developmental tasks.

For the purposes of this volume, the family will be defined as a unit with an identity of its own that is greater than that of its individual members. It is, in itself, a basic unit of emotional development that undergoes identifiable and predictable phases. That is, the family goes through its own life cycle as it progresses from the birth of the first child to the growth of grandchildren (Carter and Goldrick 1980). In addition, the family has structure, in that individual members have different roles and responsibilities that change as the family ages. Typically, the nuclear family has been defined as the marital pair and any children from that union. The extended family encompassed the marital pair, both sets of parents, grandparents, aunts and uncles (Fleck 1976). However, in recent years with the increase in single-parent homes, multiple marriages, and alternate life-styles (for example, cohabitation or primary caretakers who are not the child's biological mother), these definitions may be of limited value, and making assumptions about the membership of a family may lead to misunderstandings.

THE CONCEPTS AND PRINCIPLES OF DEVELOPMENT

Concepts

Basic to all developmental theories and research are common terms and principles that help organize concepts. Particularly important is the concept of human development. Human development involves patterned, orderly, changes over time that allow the physical organism and its personality to become fuller, bigger, and better. This process includes changes in structure, thought, and/or behavior due to both biological and environmental influences (Blocker 1966;

3

Brody and Axelrod 1975; Chinn 1974; Craig 1976). Four processes that influence development are growth, aging, maturation, and learning. Growth is defined as an increase in size or quantity to some point of optimal maturity; aging is the biological evolution beyond that optimal point (Chinn 1974). Growth occurs through hypertrophy, the increase in the size of cellular structures, or hyperplasia, the increase in the number of cells (Guyton 1971). Growth can be either incremental or replacement. Incremental growth refers to maintaining an excess in growth over normal daily losses from catabolism due to bodily processes such as perspiration, urination, or oxidation in the lungs. The increases in weight and height that occur as a child matures are examples of incremental growth. Replacement growth refers to normal refills of essential body components necessary for survival. For example, once a red blood cell (erythrocyte) has entered the cardiovascular system, it circulates for an average of 120 days before disintegrating and being replaced by another red blood cell (Guyton 1971).

Maturation and learning are closely interrelated. Maturation involves genetic potential, the preprogrammed changes that comprise alterations in a human being's structure and form, complexity, organization, and function. Learning is the process of gaining specific knowledge or skill as a result of experience, training, and behavior changes. Learning is limited by the level of maturation; the organism must be capable of making a new behavior before that behavior can be learned. For example, a child cannot be taught to walk until his or her leg muscles mature to the level of strength and coordination needed for walking.

General Principles

Although the processes underlying growth are extremely complex, human development proceeds in accordance with a number of general principles. The first of these principles is that growth and changes in behavior are orderly and usually occur in unvarying sequences. For example, all fetuses can turn their heads before they can extend their hands. After birth, there are definite patterns of physical growth and increases in motor and cognitive abilities. Every child sits before standing, stands before walking, draws a circle before drawing a square. All babies go through the same sequence of stages in speech development, babbling before talking, pronouncing certain sounds before others. Likewise, certain cognitive abilities invariably precede others; all children can categorize objects or put them into a series according to size before than can think logically or formulate hypotheses (Mussen 1973).

The second principle is that of discontinuity of growth rate. Although development is patterned and continuous, it is not always smooth and gradual (Mussen 1973). There are periods of very rapid physical growth—growth spurts—and of extraordinary increments in psychological abilities. For example, the height and weight of an infant increase dramatically during the first year, and adolescents tend to grow rapidly as well. The genital organs develop very slowly during childhood, but very rapidly during adolescence. During the preschool period, the child displays sharp increases in vocabulary and motor skills, and during adolescence the individual's ability to solve logical problems undergoes remarkable change.

The third principle is that of differentiation. Development proceeds from simple to complex, homogeneous to heterogeneous, and general to specific (Klauger and Klauger 1974). Differentiation from simple to complex motor skills occurs after birth as the infant first uses arms to wave and later learns to control finger movements. The general body configurations of males and females tend to be much more similar at birth than during late adolescence—an example of development from homogeneity to heterogeneity. General to specific development is observed in motor responses, which are diffuse and undifferentiated at birth and become more specific and controlled later on: Stimulation will result in a whole body movement in an infant; later only specific body parts will respond.

The fourth principle of development is the cephalocaudal principle. Cephalocaudal (head to tail) means that the upper end of the organism develops sooner and faster than the lower end (Murray and Zentner 1979). Increases in neuromuscular size and maturation of function begin in the head and proceed to the hands and feet. For example, pictures taken of a 5-week-old embryo over several days clearly show extensive head growth (caused mainly by development of the brain), which is accompanied by further elongation of the body structure from head to tail. After birth an infant will also be able to hold its head erect before being able to sit or walk.

The final two principles of development are those of proximodistal and bilateral development. Proximodistal (near to far) means that growth progresses from the central axis of the body

5

toward the periphery or extremities. Bilateral (side to side) means that the capacity for growth and development of the organism is symmetrical: Growth that occurs on one side of the body occurs simultaneously on the other.

These six principles of development are important at all stages of the life span—prenatal through old age.

DEVELOPMENTAL THEORISTS

As a scientific area of study, developmental psychology is less than a century old, but the questions it raises are ancient ones. Many classical philosophers wrote about the characteristics of children and theorized about the determinants of development. Mussen (1973, p. 2) wrote:

> Plato, writing in the third century B.C., recognized that individual differences in ability are, to some extent, inborn, but he also realized that early childhood training helps to determine later vocational choice and adjustment. The seventh-century English philosopher John Locke believed that strict early discipline was critical for the development of self-discipline and self-control, which in his opinion were cardinal virtues. Jean-Jacques Rousseau, the eighteenth-century French philosopher, agreed with Locke that the experiences of the first few years are crucial in a person's development. He did not, however, believe in early discipline; rather, he advocated permitting children to express their "natural impulses" freely, because he believed these impulses were inherently noble and just.

Within the field of psychology, many theorists have contributed to the study of human development; the result is a rich area of research covering several aspects of behavior change. Concepts of behaviorism and learning initially established by John Watson (1914), Ivan Pavlov (1927), and B. F. Skinner (1938) lead to the early work of Mary Cover Jones (1924) on learning in children, as well as to several theories on childhood development. Among them are the theories of Dollard and Miller (1950), Sears (1951), Bijou and Baer (1961), and Bandura and Walters (1963). Other theoretical perspectives, based on a psychoanalytic approach, have expanded developmental research beyond the childhood stages. Anna Freud (1948) has written about the psychological effects of puberty and adolescence on further adulthood development, and adulthood issues of personality development have been explored as well, initially by Harry Stack Sullivan (1953) and Alfred Adler (1971). Among the first of the psychoanalytic theorists to propose that development occurred beyond adolescence and throughout the life span was Carl Jung (1959). The contributions of these theorists have been extensive and warrant serious study. For our purposes, however, I will limit discussion to three of the most widely read theorists of developmental psychology: Sigmund Freud, who did his early work on childhood stages of personality development; Jean Piaget, who contributed to an understanding of cognitive development; and Erik H. Erikson, who wrote about the psychosocial stages of development from infancy through old age.

Sigmund Freud

One of the most appealing and natural ways to conceptualize our own behavior and that of other people has been to try to determine the intention of each act, to discover the subjective, internal processes. This notion of intention behind action is the basis of psychoanalytic or Freudian theory. *What* we do is available to anyone who chooses to observe (and is the focus of behavioral theorists), but *why* we do something can be answered, according to Freud, only by examining our past histories and our present psychological states. Consequently, early childhood development is the basis for future adult behavior. Although the specific developmental issues that occur during each stage will be discussed later on, a brief overview of the major characteristics of Freud's position is necessary as general background information.

First, psychoanalytic theory takes a deterministic point of view. Freud held that all behavior is determined or caused by some force within us and therefore all behavior has meaning. Second, as with Erikson and Piaget, Freud's view is dynamic. That is, in order to have a full understanding of personality, you must have a statement of the source of motivation for human actions. Freud postulated that this source of motivation was a unitary power or energy source found within the individual, called libido. Libido is defined as the psychic energy behind sexual instincts. (In this context, "sex" refers to almost all pleasurable actions and thoughts, not just erotic activity.) It is the energy of all mental activity and can build up pressure in much the same way as water trapped in a series of pipes with no external outlet. Consequently, reduction of this libidinal tension is necessary for an individual's functioning. Whether the release of this tension occurs through socially appropriate or destructive means depends on the moderation of the id, ego, and superego.

The third characteristic of Freudian theory—that it is a systematic view of personality—may be seen in the framework of id, ego, and superego. The id is present at birth and houses the individual's libido—untamed, animal-like drives. The superego represents the influences of society (initially the morals of the parents) and is developed slowly over the course of the individual's childhood and adolescence. The dynamic interaction or conflict between these structures is modulated by the third structure, the ego. As a person ages, the ego develops an increasing number of strategies for controlling id-superego conflicts. These strategies are called ego defenses.

A fourth characteristic of Freudian theory is that it presents a developmental point of view. Freud held that human development follows a more or less set course that consists of a series of stages through which all of us must pass. At each stage predictable id-superego conflicts must be resolved by the ego using ego defenses. If a conflict is successfully resolved at one stage, enough psychic energy (libido) remains to handle future stages. If a conflict is poorly resolved, less psychic energy is available to handle future conflicts.

Freud's theory is the basis for Erikson's life-span approach and has characteristics in common with Piaget's theory of cognitive development. In addition, Freudian theory provides the conceptual basis for a variety of psychological and psychiatric interventions and techniques often utilized in hospital settings. In this volume, Freudian theory will prove a basis for viewing the research on personality development for each age group. Some of this research supports Freud's views; some of it contradicts or challenges his theoretical framework.

Jean Piaget

Like Freud, Piaget was interested in the intention behind behavior. He also took a developmental perspective, believing that every individual must progress through a sequence of stages, each of which becomes the basis for the next. However, unlike Freud, who felt that the drive behind behavior is an animal-like, pleasure-seeking urge (libido), Piaget believed that people have a drive (biologically based) to adapt, adjust, and cope with the environment. Consequently, Piaget focused on cognitive development and the continuing interaction between environmental stimulation and cognitive abilities. Piaget's stages are primarily descriptive rather than explanatory. Unlike Freud, he does not explain pathology or how to facilitate or improve cognitive abilities. Rather he attempts to describe, through observation and examples, the capabilities and limitations of children as they develop cognitive skills in an orderly, predictable sequence.

Basic to Piaget's theory are the concepts of schema and operation. Piaget defines a schema as an organized pattern of behavior that consists of meaningful and repeatable habits. A schema involves activity – what the child does. One example of a schema is sucking in infants. According to Piaget, the child learns to repeat this activity because it results in adapting to the environment by obtaining food. The concept of an operation is more advanced and sophisticated. An operation, according to Piaget, involves mental activity or what we understand to be thinking processes. Like schemas, operations are organized and meaningful, resulting in better adaptation to the environment. Two processes promote the development of schemas and operations: assimilation and accommodation. Both processes are of equal importance and must always occur together in a mutually dependent way (Flavell 1977). Assimilation is the mental process of experiencing an event in terms of past (internal) experience. That is, people conceive of an event in terms of their existing way of thinking. An experience is then incorporated, without a break of continuity, into a person's ongoing way of thinking, a way permitted by his or her present understanding. In short, assimilation is understanding the new in terms of what is already known (Maier 1978). Accommodation, on the other hand, involves the impact of the environment upon the individual. To accommodate is to adjust, to change an earlier conception in order to fit it more correctly into the demands of the actual event. In short, accommodation is understanding a new experience in such a way that it can alter the previous understanding (Maier 1978). Consequently the individual changes and develops, becoming more capable at organizing experiences. Every interaction requires an individual to think, to feel, and to act as previous experience dictates; and with each new interaction the individual is

9

always challenged by environmental experience to think, to feel, and to act according to the impact of the new situation. Because this process is orderly and predictable, everyone progresses through stages in the same order.

When studying Piagetian theory, it is important to remember three principles. First, each stage is based on the skills and abilities of the previous stage. Second, although children may differ in the rates at which they pass through the stages of cognitive development, every child must progress through the stages in the same sequence or order. Finally, each stage is typified by the most recently emerging capability of the individual. However, the behaviors and processes that preceded the new behavior continue to occur and may even occur with greater intensity and frequency than behaviors that were most recently acquired.

As in the case of Freud, some developmental researchers have challenged Piaget's views. However, his theory still remains a useful tool for assessing the cognitive capabilities and limitations of children of various ages. Some theorists (Gellert 1962; Nagy 1959; and Steward and Regalbuto 1975) have expanded Piaget's work to provide the health professional with a framework for assessing children's understandings of medical procedures, illness, and death.

Erik H. Erikson

Erikson's theory, like the theories of Freud and Piaget, is developmental and presents an ordered sequence of stages. Although greatly influenced by Freud, Erikson tended to de-emphasize the biological and sexual determinants of behavior and to focus upon social development. In his view, the ego, not the id, is the life force for human development. He accepts the existence of an unconscious motivation, called the innate inner self. It is this inner self that interacts with the ego and both influence social behaviors. Erikson's theory is more optimistic than Freud's, in that he views every personal and social crisis as furnishing components that are conducive to growth. Whereas Freud made his inquiry within the confines of pathological development, Erikson focused on the potential of successful resolution of developmental crises.

Erikson outlined eight stages of psychosocial development, each of which represents an encounter with society. Each stage is designated by a conflict between two alternate ways of handling the encounter, one adaptive and the other maladaptive. In a sense, all of the eight conflicts are present at birth, although they come to the fore at different periods of life. At these times they must be resolved so that the individual may be fully prepared for the next major conflict. Unlike Piaget and Freud, Erikson recognized that development occurs throughout the entire life span, rather than ending primarily at the completion of adolescence. Beginning with birth and progressing through old age, his eight psychosocial crises are: basic trust versus mistrust; autonomy versus shame and doubt; initiative versus guilt; industry versus inferiority; identity versus role confusion; intimacy versus isolation; generativity versus stagnation; and ego integrity versus despair (Erikson 1963). This framework provides a helpful conceptualization for social development. In addition, the life-span approach, including adulthood, is supported by more recent research on adulthood changes (Kimmel 1980).

Although all three theorists focus on development through an orderly progression of stages, and each is deterministic in outlook, certain differences remain that are of particular importance. Each theory is grounded in a different set of assumptions with a different emphasis — Freud's on personality development, Piaget's on cognitive development, and Erikson's on social development. As stated earlier, development in one of these areas interacts and influences development in another. Each theory contains a partial or different answer concerning a child's development. But a child is not a dissected being, and if children are to be helped toward successful growth they must be viewed in light of their total development. Adherence to just one of these viewpoints is apt to result in an incomplete approach despite the fact that each theory is far richer and more complex than can be presented within the limits of this volume. I encourage you to further explore the work of these theorists through their own writings: Erikson 1963, 1968; Flavell 1977; Freud 1950, 1951, 1960, 1961, 1963; Piaget 1926, 1968; and Piaget and Inhelder 1969.

METHODOLOGICAL ISSUES

Research in developmental psychology, as in other sciences, requires systematic observation in order to support or reject a theoretical premise. It is important to understand the methods used

11

in the developmental research that supports or challenges the theories presented if you plan on forming your own evaluations of the findings.

The Concept of Statistical Normalcy

Some important research about behaviors or attitudes has consisted of surveys involving large numbers of individuals. The results of these large-scale surveys are often given as frequency ratings. For example, as early as 1877, Bowditch took weight and height measurements of boys and girls attending school in Boston and produced the first charts of average heights and weights for children of school age in the United States. Children who were significantly shorter or taller than other children their age were seen as falling outside the statistical norm. In a sense they can be viewed as "statistically deviant" (rare) in height. It is important in reviewing similar studies not to confuse statistical normalcy (commonness) with the concept of psychological normalcy. Conversely, statistical deviancy or rarity should not be confused with psychopathology, which implies malfunction. Because a behavior or attitude is not displayed by most people does not mean that it is pathological.

Experimental Design

Research studies can vary in type of setting (naturalistic, laboratory), number of subjects (case history, survey), and method of intervention (longitudinal, cross-sectional). The fundamental goal of all these methods is unbiased observation. Each has different advantages and disadvantages that influence the interpretation and applicability of the results.

Type of Setting. Observations may be made in naturalistic settings such as the home, nursery school, playground, park, or the waiting room of a doctor's office. Making observations in such settings often results in the subjects being less uncomfortable, less aware of being observed. Unfortunately, the setting is less controlled, and it is sometimes difficult to assess what factors of the setting are influencing behaviors. For example, some studies have found that people's moods can be influenced by such subtle factors as the colors of the walls (Insko and Schopler 1972). Observations made under standardized conditions such as the laboratory, which is under the control of the investigator, can be more precise and objective. The factors the investigator wishes to evaluate can be manipulated; extraneous factors, such as room color, can be held constant for all subjects. In such studies, however, there is greater risk of artificiality, and the subject's awareness of being observed may alter the results somewhat.

Subject Selection. The case history is a research design in which one individual is studied extensively. This method was the basis for the early works of Freud, Piaget, and Darwin. It is a good method to use when beginning to study a new area since it allows for the easy collection of a great deal of information that would be prohibitively expensive or time consuming to gather from many subjects. Once important variables or processes are gleaned from these large amounts of information, the variables can then be examined more systematically. In addition, the case history is often the only reasonable method to use with rare cases, such as split personalities or Siamese twins. The weakness of this method lies in its subjectivity and lack of generalizability. Survey research, at the other extreme, often involves the study of hundreds of subjects. Such studies are valuable for generalizability and for identifying trends. However, only a limited number of variables can be explored on such a large scale. Most research in developmental psychology involves studies that fall somewhere between these two extremes, with the number of subjects being determined by the number of variables being examined and the number of different interventions used.

Longitudinal and Cross-sectional Methods. Because developmental psychology is concerned with changes in behavior over time, these two types of approaches are frequently used. They can best be explained as contrasting methods. In the longitudinal approach the same group of individuals is studied, tested, and observed repeatedly over an extended period of time. For example, in investigating the development of cognitive abilities between the ages of 3 and 12 longitudinally, the investigator would gather a group of subjects and give them appropriate tests, first when they were 3 years old and subsequently at annual or semiannual intervals until they were 12. Analysis of the results of the tests would permit the definition of age trends in the development of cognitive functions. A cross-sectional approach, however, would involve giving the tests all at once to children of different ages – to samples of 3-year-olds, 4-year-olds, 5-year-olds, and so forth. Comparison of the performances of children of different ages would result, as in the longitudinal study, in descriptions of age trends in cognitive abilities (Mussen 1973).

The longitudinal approach can have several advantages over the cross-sectional method. Indeed, there are several kinds of problems that can only be adequately investigated by means of this method. For example, whether personality, intelligence, or performance are stable, or consistent, over long periods of time can only be determined if the same individuals are tested at different ages. Latent or delayed effects of early experiences (such as the effects of parental overprotectiveness on the adult personality) must also be studied longitudinally. This method can measure small changes and rates of change that might be lost in cross-sectional studies, such as how fast adolescents grow in height between age 12 and age 13. Finally, particularly in studies of adulthood and aging, the longitudinal approach avoids the distorting effects of changes in society that can occur with cross-sectional studies. For example, individuals who have lived through the depression will have different attitudes about spending money than those who did not. Consequently, comparing 80-year-olds with 20-year-olds at the same time in a cross-sectional study will result in a difference of attitudes toward spending money that might have erroneously been attributed to age change. Disadvantages of the longitudinal approach include the tendency of such studies to be very expensive and require a major time commitment, the fact that effects of repeated testing may produce some artificial results, the possibility of population losses that can threaten the study, and the fact that investigators cannot utilize new measures or techniques once such a study begins. Cross-sectional studies are faster and cheaper, do not run the risk of population loss, and produce findings that can be immediately interpreted. For example, if cross-sectional testing provided information on the effects of television violence on children of different ages, the results could lead to immediate changes in programming.

The major studies covered in this volume will be described using the variables of type of setting, number of subjects, and longitudinal or cross-sectional methods so that results can be evaluated within a sophisticated frame of reference.

SUMMARY

As stated in the beginning of this chapter, the goal of the study of human development is to obtain a complete picture of the sequence of age-related changes that occur within a lifetime. This is important to the health professional in determining what should be expected of an individual of a particular age and in understanding how concepts of illness and health interface with individual development. Such age-related changes must be understood within the context of past experiences, other developing competencies, and the social network.

The concepts and principles that are basic to all development have been presented, including the concepts of growth, aging, and maturation and the principles of orderly, discontinous, differential, cephalocalidal, proximodestal, and bilateral development. Also reviewed were the basic assumptions and foundations of the developmental theorists, primarily Freud, Piaget, and Erikson. Finally, the methodological issues that govern developmental research, specifically the concept of statistical normalcy and the effects due to setting, number of subjects, and method of intervention were discussed.

The rest of this volume will be organized according to age groups. Within this format, topics common to all ages will be presented—family; sexuality; physical, cognitive, and identity development; and special health care considerations.

REFERENCES

Adler, A. The Practice and Theory of Individual Psychology. New York: Humanities Press, 1971.

Bandura, A., and Walters, R. Social Learning and Personality Development. New York: Holt, Rinehart & Winston, 1963.

Bijou, S., and Baer, D. Child Development. Vol. 1. New York: Appleton-Century-Crofts, 1961.

Blocker, D. Developmental Counseling. New York: The Ronald Press, 1966.

Bowditch, H. P. Massachusetts State Board of Health Annual Report, 1877, 8:275-324.

Brody, S., and Axelrod, S. "Ego formation in infancy," in W. Sze (Ed.), Human Life Cycle. New York: Jason Aronson, 1975.

Carter, E., and Goldrick, M. The Family Life Cycle: A Framework for Family Therapy. New York: Gardner Press, 1980.

Chinn, P. Child Health Maintenance. St. Louis: C. V. Mosby Co., 1974.

Craig, G. Human Development. Englewood Cliffs, N.J.: Prentice-Hall, 1976.

Dollard, J., and Miller, N. E. Personality and Psychotherapy. New York: McGraw-Hill, 1950.

Erikson, E. H. Childhood and Society. 2nd Ed. New York: Norton, 1963.

_____. *Identity: Youth and Crisis.* New York: Norton, 1968.

Flavell, J. H. *Cognitive Development.* Englewood Cliffs, N.J.: Prentice-Hall, 1977.

Fleck, S. "A general systems approach to severe family pathology." *American Journal of Psychiatry,* 1976, 133(6):669–673.

Freud, A. *The Ego and the Mechanism of Defense.* Translated by C. Baines. New York: International Universities Press, 1948.

Freud, S. *The Ego and the Id.* London: Hogarth, 1950.

_____. *Psychopathology of Everyday Life.* Translated by A. A. Brill. New York: New American Library, 1951.

_____. *Jokes and Their Relation to the Unconscious.* Vol. 8. Edited and translated by J. Strachey. New York: Norton, 1960.

_____. *The Interpretation of Dreams.* Edited and Translated by J. Strachey. New York: Science Editions, 1961.

_____. *Introductory Lectures on Psycho-analysis.* Vol. 15. Edited and translated by J. Strachey. London: Hogarth Press, 1963.

Gellert, E. "Children's conceptions of the content and functions of the human body." *Genetic Psychology Monographs,* 1962, 65:293–405.

Guyton, A. *Textbook of Medical Physiology.* 4th Ed. Philadelphia: W. B. Saunders, 1971.

Insko, C. A., and Schopler, J. *Experimental Social Psychology.* New York: Academic Press, 1972.

Jones, M. C. "A laboratory study of fear: The case of Peter." *Pedagogical Seminar,* 1924, 31:308–315.

Jung, C. *Collected Works.* Vol. IX, Part 1, *The Archetypes and the Collective Unconscious.* Princeton: Princeton University Press, 1959.

Kimmel, D. C. *Adulthood and Aging.* 2nd Ed. New York: John Wiley and Sons, 1980.

Klauger, G., and Klauger, M. *Human Development: The Span of Life.* St. Louis: C. V. Mosby Co., 1974.

Maier, H. W. *Three Theories of Child Development.* New York: Harper & Row, 1978.

Murray, R. B., and Zentner, J. P. *Nursing Assessment and Health Promotion Through the Life Span.* 2nd Ed. Englewood Cliffs, N.J.: Prentice-Hall, 1979.

Mussen, P. H. *The Psychological Development of the Child.* 2nd Ed. Englewood Cliffs, N.J.: Prentice-Hall, 1973.

Mussen, P. H., Conger, J. J., and Kagan, J. *Child Development and Personality.* 4th Ed. New York: Harper & Row, 1974.

Nagy, M. "The meaning of death." In H. Feifel (Ed.), *The Meaning of Death.* New York: McGraw-Hill, 1959.

Pavlov, I. P. *Conditioned Reflexes.* New York: Leveright, 1927.

Piaget, J. *The Language and Thought of the Child.* New York: Harcourt, Brace, 1926.

———. *On the Development of Memory and Identity.* Barre, Mass.: Clark University Press and Barre Publishers, 1968.

Piaget, J., and Inhelder, B. *The Psychology of the Child.* New York: Basic Books, 1969.

Sears, R. R. "A theoretical framework for personality and social behavior." *American Psychologist,* 1951, 6(9):476–483.

Skinner, B. F. *The Behavior of Organisms.* New York: Appleton-Century-Crofts, 1938.

Steward, M., and Regalbuto, B. A. "Do doctors know what children know?" *American Journal of Orthopsychiatry,* 1975, 45:146–149.

Sullivan, H. S. *Interpersonal Theory of Psychiatry.* New York: Norton, 1953.

Watson, J. B. *Behavior: An Introduction to Comparative Psychology.* New York: Holt, 1914.

PRENATAL THROUGH
INFANCY DEVELOPMENT

INTRODUCTION

The fascination with the effects of early infancy upon latter development is an ancient one. For a long time, infants were thought to be passive, incompetent, confusing beings that people would "do things to" in order to mold them into functioning adults. William James described infants as devoid of coherent thoughts and developed senses, "a blooming, buzzing mass of confusion." Similarly, John Locke believed that infants enter the world as tabulae rasae, completely open for the experiences of life. The emphasis was on what caretakers should do to infants rather than on what infants were capable of doing themselves. As early as the fourth century, Plato was advising mothers to keep their infants in motion and to rock them to sleep rhythmically to promote the harmonious coordination of mind and body in adulthood (Jaeger 1944). More recent study finds that infants are much more equipped to handle the world at birth than was previously believed (Kopp and Parmelee 1979); in addition, we now know they are more complex and active in relating to the world (Osofsky and Connors 1979). Researchers have also discovered that the infant's capabilities are greatly influenced by prenatal and perinatal events (Kopp and Parmelee 1979). Consequently, although this stage of life only spans 22 months (compared to 10 years of adolescence), it is rich in important information for the health professional. There is great potential for the prevention of future problems in the education of expectant parents. The birth of a child also provides a unique opportunity for the health professional to be involved with the family at a time when the major focus is a natural event rather than illness.

19

In this chapter, the term prenatal will refer to the time and events prior to birth. Perinatal defines those events or conditions that involve the birthing process. The term embryo will be used for the young organism during the first three months in the womb and the term fetus for the organism from the end of the third month until birth. The term neonate defines the newborn for the first 4 weeks of life; infant refers to the first 12 months. Those responsible for the child's care and long-term welfare will be called caretakers or parental figures. These roles are often filled by the biological mother and father, but may also be filled by extended family members or individuals who are responsible for daily care of the child while the parents work outside the home.

Developmental Tasks

The following developmental goals should be accomplished by the completion of the prenatal-infancy stage:

1. Attainment of the necessary level of physical development prior to birth.
2. Physiological stability (equilibrium) after birth.
3. Awareness of what is alive and familiar.
4. Development of a feeling of and desire for affection and response from others.
5. Management of new physical changes, new motor skills, and the establishment of a rest-activity rhythm.
6. The understanding and control of the physical environment through exploration.
7. The direction of emotional expression to indicate needs and wishes and the establishment of preverbal communication.

THE FAMILY

We are beginning with the study of the family for several reasons: No person can be adequately understood without the context of the family; the family molds and shapes the individual's emotional and physical growth, and for the newborn the family is the setting in which basic trust is established (Lofgren 1981). In some respects, the life span of a family begins with the birth of the first child (Carter and Goldrick 1980). What occurs during prenatal development, delivery, and much of the first year depends a great deal on the feelings, stresses, and family history of the parental figures. Consequently, this discussion will focus on pregnancy, delivery, and the first year from the parents' perspective, describing their newly acquired roles and their relationships to each other and the child. In later sections, the infant's role in soliciting behavior from and communicating with the parental figures will be presented.

Pregnancy and Delivery

Pregnancy allows the parents time to prepare for the birth, to readjust their relationship, and to acquire new roles. Murray and Zentner (1979, p. 38) state that, "Becoming a parent involves the loss of one's own childhood and former life-style. . . . Being aware of the tremendous influence of parents on their children's development, parents may feel challenged to become the best persons they are capable of being." Kennell, Voos, and Klaus (1979) propose the following sequence of steps in the psychological adjustment to the birth of the child: (1) planning the pregnancy, (2) confirming the pregnancy, (3) accepting the pregnancy, (4) awareness of fetal movement, (5) accepting the fetus as an individual, (6) birth, (7) seeing the baby, (8) touching the baby, (9) caretaking.

It has been suggested that pregnancy is a developmental crisis for the mother involving two specific adaptive tasks. The first is the acceptance of the fetus as on integral part of herself and the second, which usually occurs with the initial sensation of fetal movement, is the awareness of the fetus as a separate individual. Attitudes that the mother has toward delivery are often influenced by her husband's support, her mother's attitudes, and complications during pregnancy. Some research has found that mothers who remain relaxed during labor and who cooperate and have good rapport with those caring for them are more apt to be pleased with their infants at first sight (Mussen 1970).

Effects of maternal behavior on the development of the fetus will be discussed later in this chapter in the section on physical development. Early attachment issues that arise right after birth will be discussed in the section on personality development.

Effects of Pregnancy on the Marital Relationship

The birth of the first child has been reported to cause an intense or severe crisis in the marriage of a majority of couples asked (Le

Masters 1971). Although couples describe the pregnancy as a source of great pride and satisfaction, they also report that the demands for providing for the infant, of cooperating in the care of another being, can lead to marital conflicts. As these tensions are resolved or maintained extreme effects on sexuality may occur within the relationship. Historically and culturally there have been many taboos against sex during both prenancy and the post-partum period (Feldman 1981). In most cases, except for approximately four weeks after delivery, no physiological restrictions are placed on sexual activity (Kolodny, Masters and Johnson 1979). Unfortunately, health professionals rarely inform couples as to how to be sexually intimate during pregnancy. A recent study (Wolman and Money 1980) indicated that of 200 women, 29 percent were instructed to abstain 2 to 8 weeks prior to delivery, 10 percent were advised about more comfortable positions, and only 2 percent were given information about alternative activities. Often couples report fears that orgasms may be harmful and induce miscarriage or labor, that the fetus will be harmed or infected, or that intercourse will be physically uncomfortable or painful (Feldman 1981). Women often report an increase in sexual tension and activity during the second trimester, but typically sexual interest falls off, especially during the last trimester. Usually women report strong needs for affection during pregnancy and desire to be held and touched (Feldman 1981).

Role of Father

In the nineteenth century, society was structured so that the father often worked as a skilled tradesman, farmer, or shopkeeper at or near his home. It was easy for him to have frequent close interactions with growing children. These conditions are quite rare today. Furthermore, men, unlike women, do not undergo an extensive social preparation for parenthood, even though pregnancy is as crucial a time for them. In fact, the social denial of permission for men to become emotionally committed to childbearing and child rearing has made many fathers believe that they are unnecessary participants in pregnancy and birth (Biller and Meredith 1975).

The father's experience in accepting the pregnancy is similar to that of the mother. The three most outstanding events in this process are: confirmation of the pregnancy, awareness of the first fetal movement, and awareness of the first obvious physical changes in the pregnant woman (Phillips and Anzalone 1978). Also, as for the mother, the pregnancy provides additional stress. Arnstein (1972) reported arrest rates for sex offenses were significantly higher for expectant fathers. Wainright (1966), in a review of ten case histories, found fatherhood to be a precipitating factor in mental disorders in men who had personality makeups that were vulnerable. Often, at the same time that he is becoming a father, the man must be concerned about additional financial responsibilities as well as adjusting to the change in his partner's role from wife and lover to mother (Phillips and Anzalone 1978). Finally, there is sometimes competition between fathers and mothers in the care of their infant. With the intervention of health professionals, however, many husbands comment on a feeling of closeness to their wives, often associated with the infant's presence.

Family issues involving the process of the birth of a child provide a rich area for the intervention of the health professional as educator, assessor of crisis points, and facilitator of psychological support.

PHYSICAL DEVELOPMENT

Prenatal and infant physical development has long been fascinating to theorists and researchers. Increasingly sophisticated research technology (Porges 1979) has changed our view of the physical capabilities of the neonate and infant. Clearly, the behavior of the young baby is far more sophisticated and complex than we had previously acknowledged. Briefly, this section will review prenatal development, influences on prenatal growth, the birth process, the capabilities of the neonate, and physical development during the first year of life.

Prenatal Development

Development is a continuous process that begins at the moment the mother's egg or ovum is fertilized by a sperm from the father. Immediately following conception, the process of mitosis, or cell division, takes place. The fertilized ovum, a single cell containing the genetic history of both parents, divides and subdivides rapidly until millions of cells have been formed. Following the principle of differentiation, as development proceeds the new cells assume highly specialized functions, becoming parts of various body systems—nervous, skeletal, muscular, or circulatory. The cephalocaudal direction of development of form and function occurs—the fetus' arm buds (the beginnings of arms) appear before leg buds, and the fetus' head is well developed before legs are well formed. The sequence of development in the prenatal period is fixed and invariable. The head, eyes, trunk, arms, legs, genitals, and internal organs develop in the same order and at approximately the same prenatal ages in all fetuses. The average full-term human pregnancy has a duration of 280 days, commonly (but not accurately) referred to as a 9-month period of 3 trimesters. Although the organism is both growing and developing throughout all phases of pregnancy, a basic classification system can be applied. The first trimester is primarily characterized by differential development of basic structures; during this time the beginning of the development of all internal organs, appendages, and sense organs occurs. The second trimester is characterized both by further development and by growth; the organism increases from 3 to 12 inches in length and from one to 24 ounces in weight. The third trimester is predominated by growth, in these last 3 months, the fetus gains about 8 inches in length and 6 pounds in weight (Osofsky 1979).

Fetal growth and development are dependent upon maternal endocrine and metabolic adjustments during pregnancy. The placenta helps to provide necessary estrogens, progesterone, and gonadotropin to sustain pregnancy and trigger other endocrine adjustments that primarily involve the pituitary, adrenal cortex, and thyroid. Fetal endocrine function is regulated independently from the mother. However, endocrine drugs given to the mother may cross the placenta and do harm to the fetus (Chinn 1974; Guyton 1971). Proliferation of neural cells occurs between 12 and 18 weeks post-conception in the human, but connections between cortical cells are still few. Intrauterine influences determine the integrity of subcortical connections, but extrauterine influences exert the major influences. The very early postnatal period is the time during which the cerebral cortex undergoes its major growth and differentiation (Osofsky 1979). A brain growth spurt, or great increase in size and complexity of cortical interconnections, occurs from the last prenatal trimester to 14 months post-term. At birth, the brain is growing at 2 mg per minute. From birth to 14 months the brain increases from .77 to 1.98 pounds. Brain growth eventually stops at 16 years of age, the endpoint for nervous system development (Eichorn 1979). The brain, like any other organ, is most vulnerable to environmental influences during its period of maximal growth. The last trimester of pregnancy through infancy is a critical period for such neurological development. ("Critical period" is a term commonly used to denote a relatively well-defined time interval when certain experiences have maximal and essentially permanent effects on behavior and/or development.) The time at which an environmental influence occurs, as well as its severity and duration, is important in considering the effect of the influence on prenatal development.

While ethical and moral considerations greatly inhibit prenatal research (particularly in humans), considerable knowledge is nevertheless available. Books by Flanagan (1962), Ingelman-Sundberg and Wirsen (1965), and Rugh and Shettles (1971) provide additional detailed presentations of prenatal growth and development.

Prenatal Influences

There are several prenatal influences that affect the state of the child at birth. The importance of these influences and the need for intervention by the health profession are underscored by the fact that death rates during the perinatal period are four times greater than those at other ages (Niswander and Gordon 1972). Of perhaps even greater significance is the broad continuum of reproductive casualty, including congenital malformations, cerebral palsy, mental retardation, deafness, blindness, and other neurosensory defects, some forms of which are thought to result from early hazards and traumas (Pasamanick and Lilienfeld 1955; Kopp and Parmelee 1979). Comprehensive medical programs directed at prevention have resulted in dramatic reductions in infant mortality rates in this country (Lesser 1972). Unfortunately, particular populations, such as the poor and adolescents, still have much higher risk rates; an infant born in a poor family still has only one-half the chance that a middle-class baby has of reaching a first birthday. (For further discussion of adolescent pregnancy, see Chapter 5.) Unfortunately, although much has been accomplished in psychological research toward gaining a general understanding of the hazards of prenatal and perinatal factors, too little is understood regarding the implications of these factors in individual diagnosis. It is assumed that early factors have enduring consequences because the same environmental influences such as poor nutrition and low socioeconomic status, appear to persist throughout childhood (Sameroff and Chandler 1977; Nelson 1981). Figure 2-1 presents a general conceptualization of the interaction of prenatal and perinatal factors with environmental factors. Several specific environmental factors that influence prenatal and subsequent development include characteristics of the mother, the effects of teratogen agents, and the mother's emotional state during pregnancy.

Maternal Characteristics. The age of the mother and number of previous pregnancies affect the health of the fetus. If the mother has had three or more pregnancies prior to age 20, the baby is less likely to be healthy. Pregnancies during adolescence more frequently result in premature birth and infant illness (Dott and Fort 1975). The factor of age is compounded by the poor diet and additional emotional stress often associated with adolescent pregnancy (see Chapter 5). Risk related to the age of the mother is least when the woman is in her twenties (Chinn 1974; Kaltreider 1976; Kopp and Parmelee 1979). The woman who becomes pregnant after age 35 runs increased risk of complications in delivery and problems in the neonate, including higher rates of infant mortality, longer labor, prematurity, low birth weight, Down's Syndrome, birth defects, and fraternal twinning (Pasamanick and Lilienfeld 1955; Mussen et al. 1974). Medical technology now allows for early detection and intervention for some of these problems (McCauley 1978). Ultrasound involves compound scanning with image reduction of the fetus and is useful for detection of fetal pulse and fetal heart movements, determination of head size in assessing growth, and localization of the placenta for amniocentesis. Amniocentesis, the withdrawal and testing of amniotic fluid from the placenta, is helpful in early diagnosis of Down's Syndrome and in predicting fetal respiratory maturity necessary prior to inducing labor or delivering by cesarean section. Equipment for con-

---

FIGURE 2-1
DEVELOPMENTAL OUTCOME

Family & Environmental Factors

		good	poor
Genetic, Prenatal, & Perinatal Factors	good	SUPERIOR	NORMAL
	poor	NORMAL	SUBNORMAL

---

tinuous fetal monitoring of heart rate and uterine activity has also been widely used prior to birth and during labor and delivery (Paul 1976).

The more pregnancies a woman has had, the greater the risk to the infant. Maternal physiology cannot support several pregnancies in quick succession (Kaltreider 1976). Research indicates that maternal age *per se* may not be as critical as the general health and dietary habits of the mother (Drillien and Ellis 1964; Ebbs et al. 1942; Kopp and Parmelee 1979; Nelson 1981; Sameroff and Chandler 1977).

The mother's health has been found to exert a potent influence over the child's prenatal development. Fetal and placental growth, nourishment, waste excretion, and total function are all dependent on the adequacy of the mother's blood system. Inadequate hemoglobin or red blood cells interfere with fetal function (Chinn 1974; Guyton 1971). In addition, infections that have a mild effect on the mother may have profound effects on the fetus, depending on gestational age (Osofsky 1979). This is particularly unfortunate as the pregnant women tends to be more susceptible to infections. The placenta is incapable of screening all infectious organisms; consequently, some infectious diseases in the vaginal region can travel to the amniotic sac, penetrate its walls, and infect the amniotic fluid. Rubella is one of the most serious diseases, especially during the first 2 or 3 months of gestation. It may go unnoticed by the mother but may cause serious congenital anomalies, particularly congenital cataract. About one in 600 children are born with congenital rubella (Chinn, 1974).

Maternal syphilis also has severe adverse effects, such as congenital syphilis, mental deficiencies, miscarriage, and stillbirth (Pasamanick and Lilienfeld 1955; Mussen et al. 1979). If maternal syphilis is not properly treated, symptoms may appear in the child at birth or up to 2 years later. Adequate treatment prior to the eighteenth week of pregnancy effectively prevents syphilis in the fetus, since the fetus appears to be relatively immune to syphilis, compared to other diseases, in early pregnancy. Penicillin and other antibiotics readily cross the placenta and, consequently, have been used to treat inuteral syphilis. Antibiotics have also been effective in treating maternal gonorrhea and other, less prevalent types of venereal disease that have varying degrees of negative effects upon the mother and her offspring (Hellman and Pritchard 1971). The diabetic mother (Mussen et al. 1979) and the women with Rh incompatibility (Kopp

27

and Parmelee 1979) are also at high risk during pregnancy and delivery and require additional medical attention.

Research on the effects of the mother's nutrition during pregnancy has been extensive. Early studies found that good diets minimize the incidence of prematurity and increase the likelihood that the child would be healthy at birth (Ebbs et al. 1942; Drillien and Ellis 1964). Poor diet was found, in animal studies, to lead to anatomical central nervous system (CNS) defects as well as increased rates of stillbirth and prematurity (Davison and Dobbing 1966; Mussen, Conger, and Kagan 1974). A pregnant woman needs about 2,000 calories more each day than a nonpregnant woman; the additional calories will result in a normal weight gain of about 25 pounds. In addition, protein requirements are 1.5 grams per kilogram daily for the pregnant woman, compared to the usual 1.0 gram per kilogram daily (Chinn 1974; Kaplan 1972). Low maternal weight at conception and little weight gain during pregnancy are associated with low-birth-weight infants who are often at high risk for other health problems. The overweight woman can jeopardize the fetus if she tries to lose weight during pregnancy; the effects of ketoacidosis resulting from calorie limitations have been associated with neuropsychological defects in infants (Ravelli, Stein, and Sussen 1962). Effects of inadequate nutrition are most severe for the pregnant adolescent who has growth requirements of her own and for the mother with the accumulated effects of several closely spaced pregnancies. Nutritional deficiencies of the mother during her own fetal and childhood periods contribute to structural and physiological difficulties in supporting a fetus. The fetus apparently draws much of its raw-material needs from maternal body structure and lifetime reserves (Chinn 1974). It was assumed in the past that socioeconomic level significantly affects the mother's nutritional status. However, according to a recent review of the literature (Eichorn 1979, p. 270), in this country "few differences were found among socioeconomic categories in the nutritional quality of the diet. . . . not only did the intake of protein and iron per 1,000 calories vary little with social class, but absolute amounts of poultry and meat consumed were similar."

Another important area for the intervention of health professionals is in treating and educating the pregnant woman. Environmental influences are often harder to deal with. Prevention involves the need for behavioral changes that are difficult to make despite our knowledge of the destructive effects at these substances (Henderson, Hall, and Lipton 1980).

Teratogen Agents. A teratogen is an agent that interrupts normal development and causes malformations. Common teratogens are radiation (x-rays) (Murphy 1929, 1947), nicotine from smoking tobacco, caffeine, alcohol, and drugs. The stage of fetal development at the time the teratogen is introduced into the mother's system determines the extent and degree of harm it causes.

As early as 1935, Sontag and Wallace showed that nicotine from cigarette smoking passes through the placenta and causes harm to the fetus. Nicotine increases fetal heart rate and contributes to fetal hyperactivity. An increased mortality rate during the first month of life, the presence of congenital heart disease, and the possibility of convulsions up to the age of 7 may result in children whose mothers smoked during pregnancy (Hellman and Pritchard 1971). Longo (1977) recently reviewed the several adverse effects of carbon monoxide (separate from nicotine) from cigarettes on the fetus. In addition, infants of smoking mothers, in comparison to infants of nonsmoking mothers, have significantly more hospital admissions with a diagnosis of bronchitis or pneumonia (Harlap and Davis 1974).

Caffeine and alcohol are also harmful to the fetus. Soyka (1979), in a review of the research on the effects of caffeine, concluded that effects occur only with extremely high doses (250 to 800 mg per kg). Animal research, which found decreases in fetal weight due to caffeine consumption used such high doses that it would be comparable to a 50-kg woman consuming 40 cups of coffee per day. A few inconclusive epidemiologic studies have been done with human subjects. Soyka concludes that "the mutagenic significance of caffeine in man is not established as being either of great concern or easily dismissable (p. 46)." Actually, research being done in Italy found that caffeine inhibited uterine activity and was a useful agent in the management of threatened abortion and premature labor (Soyka 1979). The results of the research on prenatal effects of caffeine should indicate caution, particularly since heavy coffee consumption in humans is so often associated with heavy use of alcohol and cigarettes (Rosett and Sander 1979), whose destructive effects are known.

Alcohol should be completely avoided by the pregnant woman. As little as 3 ounces of liquor daily increases the chances of congenital defects, and research indicates that effects may be intensified in the last trimester (Rosett and Sander 1979). Because chronic heavy alcohol consumption adversely affects almost every organ system in the body, many nonspecific risk factors can result from alcohol use during pregnancy. The infant may be born with fetal alcoholic syndrome (FAS), which involves malformations such as cleft palate, micropthalmia and a malformed facial profile (protruding forehead, sunken nasal bridge, short upturned nose, retracted upper lip, receding chin, and deformed ears). The child may be hyperactive, show delayed psychomotor and language development, or be intellectually retarded (Rosett and Sander 1979). The use of drugs such as heroin, methadone, LSD, barbiturates, and Dilanten has also consistently been associated with higher incidence of low-birth-weight infants, increased perinatal mortality, and infant addiction at birth (Rothstein and Gould 1974). The effects of over-the-counter medications such as aspirin and antihistamines are still being studied; the results are inconclusive (Rudolph 1981). A recent controversy surrounded Bendectin, a drug commonly prescribed to prevent nausea during pregnancy. Early studies found a higher incidence of birth defects in children whose mothers took Bendectin during pregnancy. However, these studies suffered from methodological problems, such as post-hoc investigation and self-report of drug intake. When these design problems were corrected and the studies were replicated, no relationship was found between the use of the drug and negative effects (Cordero, Oakley, Greenberg, and James 1981; Mitchell, Rosenberg, Shapiro, and Stone 1981). The effects of medications on the developing fetus are of obvious importance and require continued review of research by the health professional.

Maternal Psychological Stress. The pregnant couple, particularly vulnerable to environmental stress, is also exposed to psychological stress, which often produces physiological changes because of the sympathetic division response of the autonomic nervous system. The sympathetic nervous system is that part of the autonomic nervous system that is particularly responsive to stress reactions. For example, it directly innervates the adrenal medella, which leads to increased heart rate, muscle constriction, and tremendous metabolic effects. These reactions cause an increase in hormones and adrenalin. The hormones and adrenalin can pass through the placenta of the pregnant woman and affect the fetus. In one study, Sontag and Wallace (1935) found that movement of the fetus increased several hundred percent when the mother was under immediate stress. Long-term or chronic stress has also been found to cause physiological problems in adults (Bieliauskas, 1981). In studying pregnant women, Landis and Bolles (1947) positively correlated chronic stress during pregnancy with increased difficulty during labor.

Sameroff and Chandler (1977) emphasized the important relationship between prenatal and newborn care. Their research showed that chronic stress may lead the mother to increase her use of alcohol and drugs, including tranquilizers, during pregnancy. The negative effects on the fetus may then result in her giving birth to an irritable, unappealing infant – difficult to manage, having fussy eating habits, poor food intake, and frequent regurgitations. These characteristics are more prevalent in neglected children. In such cases, environmental effects produce prenatal deficits, which in turn solicit negative environmental effects.

Birth

Like the events that occur during pregnancy, what happens during the process of delivery can affect the physical and psychological well-being of the child. Two particular concerns for the physical health of the child involve anoxia and the effects of medications used for pain relief.

Anoxia is a decreased supply of oxygen and increased levels of carbon dioxide. There can be two major causes of anoxia during delivery: The intense pressure on the head of the infant during passage down the birth canal can cause blood vessels in the brain to rupture, or the newborn may fail to breathe properly. In both cases, the brain is deprived of oxygen, and in severe cases anoxia may result in brain damage or death. Fortunately, newborn babies are better able to withstand periods of low oxygen than are adults. In serious cases, the brain stem, which controls many integrated motor behaviors, is particularly susceptible to injury, and the anoxic newborn may show a paralysis of legs or arms, tremors of the face or fingers, or an inability to use vocal muscles properly. Long-term effects of anoxia have been debated. Longitudinal studies done over a period of 7 years have suggested that up to age 7, at least, children who were anoxic at birth perform more poorly on tests of sensorimotor and cognitive-intellectual skills than children who had normal births; the same research also indicates that they are more easily distracted.

31

Sameroff and Chandler (1977), however, argue strongly against any serious, permanent intellectual damage.

Drugs used for pain relief during childbirth cross the placenta and consequently affect the neonate. Although there is a general conviction among clinicians that the obstetrical use of drugs has decreased over the last few years, this opinion is not supported by research. Several longitudinal studies (Brackbill 1979; Hill et al. 1977; Richards 1976) found that drug administration is on the increase. One survey discovered that 95 percent of the deliveries performed at 18 teaching hospitals across the country were carried out under some form of anesthesia (Brackbill 1979). A review of the research indicates that drugs given the mother during labor and delivery cause depressive effects in the neonate. These effects are dose-related and are most severe in cases where the mother received high-potency drugs or a high total dose of several drugs. Conclusions cannot yet be drawn as to all the effects obstetrical medications may have on a newborn. In part, this is due to the limitations of past research. For example, very few studies have used nonwhite populations (Brackbill 1979). Black babies are more motorically mature at birth, and if a prime target of drug effects is motor coordination, then data from black samples would differ from data from white samples. Studies on the differential effects of medication due to race need to be done. Other unanswered questions include: What are the long-term effects of medication? What role does the length of labor play in medication use and subsequent effects on the child?

The Neonate

The neonate period of infancy includes the critical transition from parasitic fetal existence to physiological independence. This transition begins at birth with the first cry. Air is sucked in and inflates the lungs. Complex chemical changes are initiated in the cardiorespiratory system so that the neonate's heart and lungs can assume the burden of oxygenating the body. Vital signs in the newborn are not stable. An undeveloped heat-regulating mechanism allows body temperature to fluctuate from 97° to 100° F in response to the environment. An immature cardiac regulatory mechanism (in the medulla) causes the pulse to range from 120 to 150 beats per minute (compared to approximately 72–74 for adults). Respirations range from 35 to 50 per minute and are irregular, quiet, and shallow.

Blood pressure may range from 40 to 70 systolic millimeters of mercury. By one month, the pulse averages 130 beats and blood pressure averages 80/46. By 6 months the pulse averages 130 beats and blood pressure averages 90/60 (Murray and Zentner 1979).

The average birth weight of white male infants in America is 7.5 pounds; for females it is 7 pounds. Newborns of Black, Indian, and Oriental parents are on the average somewhat smaller. Prenatal factors such as maternal age, diet, or the effects of teratogens can influence birth weight. In identifying low-birth-weight infants, it is important to differentiate premature infants whose weight is appropriate for gestational age from premature and full-term infants who are markedly underweight for their gestational age. Shortly after birth the neonate loses up to 10 percent of birth weight, due to water loss. Parents should be told that this is normal and precedes a steady weight gain that begins 1 to 2 weeks after delivery.

The appearance of the newborn is sometimes a shock to parents. The newborn often has a misshapen head, flat nose, puffy eyelids, large tongue, and undersized lower jaw; short neck and small sloping shoulders; short limbs and large rounded abdomen with a protruding umbilical stump; and bowed, skinny legs. The head, which accounts for one-fourth of the total body size, appears large in relation to the rest of the body. The newborn's skin is thin, delicate, and usually mottled. It varies from pink to reddish in color and becomes very ruddy when the baby cries. If the newborn is jaundiced, the skin will be yellowish. The appearance of lanugo (fetal downy hair), vernix caseosa (protective crusty skin covering), milia (tiny white spots of sebaceous secretions often sprinkled on the nose and forehead), and hemangiomas (pink spots that appear on the face) are often disconcerting to parents but are normal and to be expected. Neonates differ in appearance, size, function, and response. Females are more developmentally advanced than males, blacks more developmentally advanced than whites (Mussen et al. 1979). The health professional can make an accurate assessment only by comparing the neonate against norms for the same sex and race.

Neonate Capabilities. Because neonates perceive their world from the moment they enter it, they must arrive with a remarkably well-developed sensory system. The newborn can see, hear, smell, and respond to touch and change of position. Sensitivity to pain, already present at birth, becomes keener within the first few days (Mussen 1973). The sense of taste is not well developed at first, but, within 2 weeks the infant can differentiate between sweet-tasting and sour-tasting substances. Coordination and convergence of the eyes, required for visual fixation and depth-perception, begin to develop immediately after birth and appear to be fairly well established by the age of 7 or 8 weeks. The neonate's definite visual preferences have been a topic of research for about 20 years. Robert Fantz (1964), a pioneering researcher in the area of neonatal perceptual development, contributed the visual preference method of determining neonatal visual activity. The neonate is presented with two different stimuli at the same time. One stimulus is a solid patch of gray and the other is identical in size but is composed of stripes. If the newborn cannot distinguish the stripes, the striped patch would look identical to the solid patch. But if the neonate can see the stripes, he will presumably spend more time looking at the striped patch because it is more interesting. The researcher might start with a patch of stripes that are, for example, one-eight of an inch wide and could then change the width of the stripes until they reach a size that the neonate can discriminate. In this way, visual activity in the newborn may be assessed. A major area of controversy in the research on neonatal perception involves evidence for special preferences for facial stimuli (Nelson 1981).

Bronson (1974) was the first to document the fact that neonates primarily use a more immature "second visual system" that integrates visual information at the level of the superior colliculus (the midbrain). This visual system dominates for the first 6 to 8 postnatal weeks and involves rod-based perceptions. Consequently, newborns are visually attracted by large bright objects with a lot of black/white or equivalent contrast. Because of this second visual system, moving objects are especially stimulating as they evoke primitive visual following reflexes or reactions that will shift the eyes toward salient peripheral stimulus. As the neonate matures, the primary or cortical visual system (from the cortex) increases in dominance and eventually processes all visual stimuli and controls visual memory. Finally, research has shown that a neonate will make defensive movements if an object looms rapidly toward the face (Ball and Tronick 1971). This response strongly suggests that the newborn perceives a three-dimensional world and has a rather sophisticated sensory-motor integration (Nelson 1981).

The neonate's auditory development is not as sophisticated as the visual development. Neural development of the auditory pathways is not complete until about 18 months of age. Nevertheless, the neonate discriminates sounds on the bases of loudness, duration, and pitch. The very young baby can easily appreciate ten decibel differences in tone, as well as the difference between a 2-second and a 10-second tone, and can discriminate pitch well enough to distinguish tones that differ by only 50 cycles per second. Neonates readily localize sound; they will turn their heads toward a continuous lateral source of sound. This activity demonstrates auditory-visual integration: The baby "expects" to see something when turning toward the sound. Such behavior is also important in encouraging social interactions of the neonate with caretakers.

In addition to these sensory capabilities the neonate is born with several types of reflexes. Consummatory reflexes, such as rooting and sucking, promote survival through feeding. Avoidance of potentially harmful stimuli occurs through sneezing, blinking, and the moro response. (The moro response is provoked by making a loud noise or startling the baby, which causes the infant to extend both arms outward with fingers spread and then bring them together in a tense quivery embrace.) Exploratory reflexes, such as smiling, are also present at birth. Recent findings in neonatal reflexes and motor behavior show significant racial differences. For instance, Oriental babies have no stepping reflex and do not struggle when the airway is occluded. Black neonates develop motor control faster than do neonates of most other races (Nelson 1981).

These first capabilities provide the neonate with a remarkable potential for learning and for developing the behaviors needed to form relationships with parental figures.

The Infant

During infancy different parts of the body grow at different rates until body proportions become more like those of an adult. In accordance with the cephalocaudal principle of development, the head and upper parts of the body grow at a faster pace than the trunk and legs. Head size increases at an amazing rate—brain size doubles during the first 2 years. The trunk ranks second to the head in overall growth rate, reaching approximately half of its full adult length by the end of the second year (Mussen 1973). The baby's birthweight doubles during the first 6 months and almost triples in the first year.

Because the endocrine system is still developing in infancy and does begin to fully function during the first 18 months, the infant is susceptible to stress, including fluid and electrolyte imbalance. This is primarily due to the small size of the adrenal gland and poor integration of adrenal cortex and pituitary gland functioning (Murray and Zentner 1979). The pituitary gland continues to secrete the growth hormone and thyroid-stimulating hormone that influence growth from the fetal stage through adolescence. In addition to the vulnerabilities caused by endocrine immaturity, the respiratory tract tissues remain small and relatively delicate and provide inadequate protection against infectious agents. Mucous membranes, which in the adult produce mucous to humidify and clean the inhaled air, are immature in the infant and produce less mucous, increasing susceptibility to infection. The close proximity of the middle ear, eustachian tube, throat, trachea, and bronchi result in rapid spread of infection from one structure to the other. By the end of the first year, however, the lining of the airway resembles that of an adult.

When the infant is approximately 3 or 4 months old, a neurodevelopmental reorganization occurs. This involves the simultaneous occurrence of rapid qualitative and quantitative changes in virtually all areas of physiology and behavior. In many respects, the 3- to 4-month-old infant is a very different person than the same child at one or 2 months of age. Usually parental figures will notice changes in eating, sleeping, and/or activity patterns. The influences of these physiological developments will be discussed later in this chapter. Table 2-1 shows the sequence of behavioral changes that results from physical development during infancy.

Physical development from conception through the first year is of primary importance to the health professional. Most interactions with families of newborns and infants involve concerns about normal physical development, adjustments to that development, and the consequences of illness on physical development. It is difficult to differentiate what we usually understand as cognitive and personality development from physical development. Researchers are often intrigued by the question of where natural endowment ends and experience begins. For example, is behavior the result of reflexes (physical development) or of thoughts (cognitive development)? Is smiling a reflex or an expression of a relationship (personality development)? It is particularly difficult to distinguish distinct physical, cognitive, and personality capabilities during the prenatal-infancy period.

TABLE 2-1
MILESTONES IN EARLY DEVELOPMENTAL TESTING

AGE	NORMAL BEHAVIOR	ABNORMAL BEHAVIOR
3 months	Good attention (head turn) Opens hands Smiling Babbling	No visual or auditory attention (even of eyes) (no smiling/ gaze aversion)
6 months	Active sensory-motor reaching and grasping Discriminates mother and family from strangers Smiling Sitting Babbling with gestures (Begins crawling or other prewalking progression)	Passive sensory-motor deficit (no head turn to sound) Hands fisted Scissoring of legs No midline hand movements Quiet (no babbling) (Does not discriminate family from strangers)
9 months	Crawling Pincer grasp Object permanence "Words" and gestures	No sitting No reaching and grabbing/no object manipulation. No vocalization (No crawling) (No discrimination of strangers)
12 months	Pulling up next to furniture, standing and walking First words Cooperates in games	No crawling No pincer grasp No imitation/no social cooperation No object permanence No discrimination of strangers (No cooperation in games)

Source: Nelson (1981).

COGNITIVE DEVELOPMENT

There has been considerable research in the area of cognitive abilities since the early 1930s, resulting in a greater respect for the capabilities of newborns and infants.

Studies of the cognitive behavior of the neonate and infant show that there are three aspects to be considered: (1) attention, (2) memory, and (3) learning capacity. An important component of attention for the neonate and infant is arousal. Because infants spend little time in an aroused state, study is difficult. Neonates sleep a total of approximately 16–17 hours a day with periods of only 4 minutes of uninterrupted wakefulness. Table 2-2 presents the six states of alert-

TABLE 2-2

NEONATAL STATES OF ALERTNESS

State 1 -- Quiet Sleep	Non-REM (rapid eye movements). Slow wave, high-voltage EEG alternating with quiescent periods. Baseline motor activity is low, but spontaneous startle responses occur at the rate of about 20 per hour.
State 2 -- Active Sleep	REM present. Characterized by low-voltage high-frequency EEG and vigorous dreaming. Twitching movements are frequent in fingers and toes.
State 3 -- Drowsiness	Characterized by desynchronized EEG, opening and closing eyes, and minimal limb movement. Visual following of a moving object is virtually impossible to elicit, and autonomic attention responses almost never occur.
State 4 -- Quiet Alertness	Characterized by open, alert eyes that engage in visual following. Psychophysiological attention and moderate limb movements are also seen.
State 5 -- Active Alertness	Limb movements are vigorous and both visual and autonomic attention responses may be more difficult to elicit.
State 6 -- Fussing and Crying	Movements are vigorous and attentive behavior is difficult or impossible to elicit.

SOURCE: Berg and Berg (1979).

ness that have been identified in the neonate. Infants' ultradian rhythm (cycles of alertness) also differs from the adult cycle. Adults have 90-minute cycles oscillating from alert to sluggish response, but the infant's cycle is only 45 minutes long. When the infant is under observation, state of arousal is important since clearly there are some states in which the infant is awake but incapable of learning.

Another component of learning is memory. There are three types of memory: perceptual, short-term, and long-term. Retrieval of material can be either through recognition or recall. No means are available to determine the extent of the infant's recall abilities. Recent research claims that even neonates can recognize their mothers; the baby's responses are significantly different when handled by its mother than they are when the baby is handled by strangers (Nelson

1981). Long-term retention of events from infancy has been rarely documented, however.

Learning Capabilities

Babies are capable of learning from the very first few days of life. Once a baby is in an attentive state, three types of learning can take place. These are: (1) habituation, (2) classical conditioning, and (3) operant conditioning. Habituation is the gradual loss of interest in a stimulus that accompanies repeated exposures. It is a demonstration of cognitive process. In order to look less at a stimulus on a later trial, the individual must remember that it was seen earlier. Classical conditioning involves the learning of a new association between unrelated stimuli and is very difficult to obtain in the neonate. One of the earliest classical conditioning studies (Mussen, Conger, and Kagan 1974) found that neonates from 2 to 9 days old exhibited sucking and mouth-opening behaviors at the sound of a buzzer that had previously been paired, over many trials, with feeding. Operant or instrumental conditioning has been much easier to accomplish in the infant and is most successful when oral responses or well-developed reflexes are modified through experience. For example, a neonate will automatically display rooting reflex when touched on the cheek at the corner of the mouth. In one study neonates learned to root to one side when they heard a positive signal paired with a touch on the cheek but withheld rooting to a touch on the cheek accompanied by a negative auditory signal (Reese and Lipsett 1970). This research showed that ongoing behaviors are easy to modify (operant conditioning), but new behaviors are much more difficult to learn (classical conditioning).

Piaget

According to Piaget's theory, the first stage of cognitive development is the sensorimotor period, extending from birth to about 18 months or 2 years of age. During this time, the child's perceptions improve and he or she performs increasingly complex actions, but does not show mental representation or thought processes that depend on symbolic language. During the first 4 months of life, according to Piaget, most behavior is reflexive, although some primitive intention is shown. From 4 to 8 months, the baby learns to initiate and recognize new experiences and to repeat pleasurable ones. The infant is capable of anticipating familiar events or the position of a moving object. By the time children reach 8 to 12 months, their responses are systematic and well organized. The 8- to 12-month-old displays goal-directed behavior, recognizes the shapes and sizes of familiar objects regardless of the perspective from which they are viewed, and recognizes someone other than self. Around the age of 9 to 12 months children master object permanence. By this cognitive process the infant realizes that objects and persons continue to exist even after they are out of sight. To test for the sense of object permanence, the researcher covers an object and observes the infant moving the cover in order to view or secure the object.

Language Acquisition

Infancy, for normal children, according to Piaget, ends with the beginning of real language. Speech is understood to be the ability to utter sounds, whereas language refers to the combination of sounds into a meaningful whole in order to communicate thoughts and feelings. Language acquisition begins with crying. This form of communication is joined by the cooing (soft murmur) and babbling (incoherent sounds made by playing with sounds) that begin in the second or third month. The number of sounds produced by babbling gradually increases, reaching a peak at 8 months. At first these vocalizations are reflexive – no difference exists between the vocalizations of hearing infants and deaf infants before 6 months of age. Later these vocalizations become self-rewarding. At every age the child has better comprehension than expression. The child first associates certain words with visual, tactile, and other sensations aroused by objects in the environment. Between 9 and 12 months, infants learn to recognize their names, the names of familiar objects, and the meaning of "no." The acquisition of language is quite complex and not completely understood although several theories propose explanations of the processes involved. The development of language skills is an important task for preschool children and will be therefore discussed more fully in Chapter 3.

Cognitive development is important in establishing attachment behaviors and in successfully adapting to the environment. The assessment of these abilities is important for early detection of mental retardation or neurological deficiency and identification of possible detrimental effects of a deprived environment.

SEXUAL DEVELOPMENT

Affectional/sexual development, in relation to other aspects of development (motor, language), has typically been repressed in Western culture. Sex is seldom treated as a strong, healthy force in the positive development of personality (Feldman 1981; Wolman and Money 1980). The fact that infants have erotic capacity and that this capacity develops in conjunction with other capabilities is often ignored or overlooked. Infancy has generally been considered asexual and childhood as a period of innocence that is broken at puberty. Recent research makes clear, however, that sexual/sensual/erotic growth develops gradually in conjunction with other maturational processes (Feldman 1981; Kolodny, Masters, and Johnson 1979). This section will focus on the process by which the fetus and infant become sensually aware of self, the role of parents in this process, and sex differences that become the basis for future sex-role identification.

Sensual Awareness

It appears that by the eighth week of gestation the fetus has intact sensory mechanisms; fetal movement then becomes crucial for development and comfort. Also, it is likely that the fetus sucks before birth (Kolodny, Masters, and Johnson 1979). Neonates do have some sexual capacity at birth. Males are often born with erections, and females show signs of vaginal lubrication. These sexual indications may be due in part to tactile experiences during birth (Kolodny, Masters, and Johnson 1979). There is evidence that newborns experience pleasure (not necessarily erotic) from genital stimulation that can often quiet and relax (Feldman 1981). In some African tribes this method is frequently used to calm infants (Wolman and Money 1980). Like early feelings of hunger, pain, and comfort, sensual/erotic sensation in the newborn probably tends to be diffuse and becomes more localized as the infant ages.

Early encounters with parental figures are important to this process of sensory/affectional development. These relationships provide important sources of contact in the discovery of body sensitivity and the growth of sexual consciousness. During the first year, the mouth is the chief focus of sensory pleasure, but infants also respond to total body contact. Sucking (both thumb and breast) is often the major tactile encounter and is accompanied by a variety of rhythmic movements that are followed by relaxation. Studies show that nursing is sexually arousing to the mother, and that mothers who choose to nurse have higher levels of sexual interest (Kolodny, Masters, and Johnson 1979). Arousal related to nursing may also produce guilt in the mother and dislike or jealousy on the part of the husband/lover, causing tension in interactions with the infant.

During the first year, the infant's sensual awareness progressively shifts to other body areas, such as feet, thighs, and abdomen. These sensations combine with the infant's own discoveries through self-exploration and become integrated into a body image. The infant becomes aware that some body parts give greater pleasure than others and that there are differences in sensation when touching its own body compared to touching another object. These experiences, however, usually depend on the acceptance and attitudes of the parents. Without adequate somatosensory stimulation, body image is impaired and pesonality development delayed, as shown by studies of premature incubator infants who lacked rocking, stroking, and cuddling (Dennis 1960; Rheingold 1956).

Sex Differences

The presence or absence of the Y chromosome at conception is the source of variance between the sexes that sometimes has subtle effects on later sex-role identification. Among the more interesting findings is that, although males, from birth onward, are taller, heavier, and progressively stronger than females, they tend to be more biologically vulnerable than females. Males have a higher mortality rate. For every 120 to 170 males conceived, only 100 females are conceived; at birth this ratio has been reduced to 105:100 male to female live births; and during the first year one-third more males than females die (Westman 1973). More males than females die at every age from conception to middle age. Males are also more vulnerable to sex-linked non-infectious diseases, such as hemophilia, hyperthyroidism, and color-vision deficits; they are three times more likely than females to have abnormalities during neonatal life; and more males than females develop learning, language, and behavior disorders. Maturation studies show that the female neonate is approximately 4 to 6 weeks ahead of the male neonate in developmental rate. This difference in rate of development becomes greater with age. Women reach their final physical maturity at approximately 21 years, an average of 3 years ahead of males (Westman 1973). Studies have consistently found that female neonates are more sensitive to tactile stimulation and pain (Murray and Zentner 1979). Researchers attribute these differences at the neonatal stage either to the greater neurological maturity of females or the higher frequency of neonatal abnormalities for males.

These sex differences elicit different responses from caretakers. For example, Moss and Robson (1967) found that mothers of male babies were initially more involved with their children and described them as more fretful and difficult to take care of. When the babies reached the age of 3 months, however, the mother of female babies become more involved, citing the social rewards of earlier smiling and vocalizations. Differences in treatment based on sex of child and sex of parent become more pronounced as the child ages.

PERSONALITY DEVELOPMENT

Because the infant is so physically dependent upon caretakers that their inattention becomes life-threatening, personality development of the first year can best be understood in the context of social relationships. Freud (1950) recognized this in his emphasis on early mother-infant relationship. The first stage of development according to Freud is the oral stage, dominant in the first 12 to 18 months of life. The infant responds to thirst and hunger by sucking, swallowing, oral-tactile stimulation, and crying. Tactile stimulation, important in cognitive and sexual development, is essential to the formation of the relationships necessary for personality development.

Like Freud, Erikson (1963) recognized that the first stage of development involved primary relationships with caretakers. The developmental crisis for infancy, according to Erikson, involves trust versus mistrust. Basic trust means confidence, optimism, reliance on self and other, faith that the world can satisfy needs, and a sense of hope or a belief in the attainability of wishes in spite of problems. This sense of trust forms the basis for later identity formation and social responsiveness to others. Conversely, mistrust is a sense of not feeling satisfied emotionally or physically. It is characterized by pessimism, lack of self-confidence, suspicion and bitterness toward others, and antagonism. Erikson maintained that the amount of trust did not depend on the absolute quantities of food or manifestations of love, but on the quality of the caring relationship. Subsequent research has supported his observations. Schaffer and Emerson (1964) found that the availability of the mother and the amount of contact she had with the child were insignificant. What did matter was that someone in the role of caretaker responded quickly to the infant's cries or demands and spontaneously initiated contact. Thus a baby might develop more trust and become more attached to an attentive, stimulating father than to an unstimulating mother, even though the mother spent more time giving routine care.

Research indicates that the hours immediately following birth may be critical for the formation of attachment feelings in the parents (Klaus and Kennell 1976; Kennell, Voos, and Klaus 1979). At birth a baby's sleep-wakefulness cycle changes. If there are no effects of obstetric medication, the baby tends to have eyes open, gazing around, and exhibits strong sucking reflexes and more physical activity (Greenberg and Morris 1974). This period of wakefulness is thought to be genetically programmed to provide a period for bonding between parents and baby. Numerous studies have shown that this early contact provides a number of positive effects. Among these are: increases in length of time breastfeeding, more interest in the baby reported by parents, less child abuse, increased verbalizations between mother and infant, and decreased crying (Kennel, Voos, and Klaus 1979). Some researchers have claimed that effects of early contact can be maintained up to 10 years of age, but this is disputed. Clearly, however, short-term effects are now well accepted; early-contact babies show better health and more weight gain than those who have been separated immediately after birth (Kennell, Voos, and Klaus 1979). This area of research is very important to health professionals. Hospitals and staff, through policies involving separation of parents and newborns immediately following birth, have great influence on the quality of early contact. Birth defects, difficulties and complications with labor, and infant sickness have been shown to have strong effects on early parental bonding (Osofsky 1979). In these special cases, informed medical care is critical.

Infant-Initiated Interactions

The neonate has a fairly rich repertoire of social behavior that is often used to initiate interactions with adults. Bell (1971; 1979), in reviewing the literature on caretaker-offspring interactions, concluded that four-fifths of interactions are initiated by the infant and that specific maternal behavior depended more on the infant's behavior than on the mother's general attitudes about parenting. Social behaviors of neonates include quieting to speech, movement in synchrony with speech, facial regard, cuddling in the nape of the neck, and imitation of facial expressions (Nelson 1981). In addition, the frequent reflexive smiles of the infant while drowsy or dreaming are often seen as socially reinforcing by caretakers.

Individual Differences

Infants have varying temperaments that influence parental interactions and confidence in parenting skills. Various observers have noted individual differences in infants' crying, irritability, and need for physical contact (Moss and Robson 1967), reactions to stimulation (Murphy 1974), and activity level (Escalona 1968). Thomas (1971) found that an infant's tendency to either seek out or withdraw from new stimuli remains stable for from 3 months to 2 years. Many of the various individual differences may be related to a difference of style in reaction to stimuli. In fact, Murphy (1974) suggests that stimulus management is one of the basic coping tasks for infants. The infant must evoke enough stimulation to foster development or perceptual-motor and cognitive functioning but ward off excessive or painful stimulation. The infant's habitual mode of regulating stimulation is the infant's temperament or personality. Escalona (1973), in her work with infants who were between 1 and 8 months old, identified babies who tended to be more active in response to stimuli and when alone and babies who were more inactive and required stimulation from others. Particularly important to health professionals is a study by Schaffer (1966) who found that hospitalization had less adverse effects on active infants than it did on inactive infants in terms of retarding development. Busy staff members might easily ignore an inactive baby, who may actually require more stimulation than an active one.

Individual differences clearly influence infant interactions with parental figures (Brazelton, Koslowski, and Main 1974). For example, a highly active caretaker who expects an intense reaction may have a difficult time mothering a low-activity, quiet baby. In such a case the infant may be overstimulated, react with fussiness or withdrawal, and the caretaker may interpret such behavior as rejection. If a parental figure thinks of a contented baby as one that can be cuddled, unfulfilled expectations may result in a sense that something is wrong or that the infant is ill.

Two other manifestations of an infant's personality are separation anxiety and stranger anxiety. Separation anxiety is defined as the distress seen between 9 and 12 months of age when the primary caretaker leaves the infant. The strength of the behavioral and physiological distress is often taken as a measure of the strength of the infant's attachment to the primary caretaker. An infant may react to the absence of more than one caretaker and usually does. Separation anxiety is explained by researchers as the infant's distress over an inability to maintain a cognitive image of the caretaker after the caretaker leaves (Mussen, Conger, and Kagan 1974). Consistency in parental behavior is an important factor in a child's response to separation. Infants who see parents leave and return at the same time each day show less separation anxiety (Mussen et al. 1979) than do children who are rarely separated from their mothers. Children who are rarely separated actually show an earlier onset of separation anxiety (Ainsworth 1969).

Stranger anxiety might be viewed as the reverse of attachment – as the tendency to avoid proximity with certain other people. In the United States, stranger anxiety appears at 7 to 9 months of age. The response is significantly attenuated if the infant has continuous exposure to a wide variety of friendly strangers and acquaintances visiting the household. The health professional can dilute the intensity of stranger anxiety by being silent and slow-moving in first encounters with infants (Schaffer 1966) and by interacting when the primary caretaker is present.

An understanding of the important issues of personality development in infants will allow the health professional to promote early bonding with parents, assess individual differences, educate caretakers in parenting skills that take these differences into account, and establish a relationship with the child that will maximize the effectiveness of health care.

HEALTH CARE CONSIDERATIONS

In addition to the various health considerations involving the family and promoting physical, cognitive, sexual, and personality development in the infant, several additional areas are of special concern to the health professional. Often the health professional must make some assessment of the capabilities of the newborn and infant in order to determine the need for referral. The professional is also involved in the important task of promoting health by preventing disease and encouraging good nutritional habits. In addition, special populations—premature infants, children born with congenital diseases, children with Down's Syndrome, and abused children—require special treatment. Finally, the health professional must often help parents grieve for the child placed in adoption, the deformed child, and the child who dies in infancy.

Assessment of the Infant

A major sign of illness in an infant is a consistent lack of attentive behavior, which must be assessed in the context of the child's arousal state and individual temperament. Four measures are commonly used to assess the attentive behavior of infants. The APGAR scoring system, developed by Virginia Apgar, is used to determine the physical status of the newborn one minute after birth and then 5 minutes later. Systematic observations are made of the newborn's respirations, heart rate, muscle tone, reflex activities, and color, resulting in a score that determines whether life-saving intervention is needed. The Brazelton Neonatal Behavioral Assessment Scale (BNBAS) is the most recent standardized test of neonatal behavior. It includes both neurological and behavioral test items. The test is not predictive of behavioral test performance later in infancy or early in childhood, but rather is the best available tool for assessing neonatal capabilities in relation to other neonates tested under the same carefully controlled conditions. The premature infant gets a poor score on the Brazelton test if it is tested before reaching term gestational age. Furthermore, no special testing procedures exist that can measure the limited response capabilities of the premature infant. Until efforts, currently under way, to develop such tests are successful (Nelson 1981), the premature infant will continue to present special problems for accurate behavioral assessment. (See Brazelton 1979 for more information on this subject.)

A third measure often used is the Denver Developmental Screening Test (DDST) to assess the behavioral competence of the infant and young child in four areas of development: gross-motor, fine-motor, language, and personal-social behavior. The test was intended to detect developmental delays between birth and 6 years of age. Finally, the Bayley Scales of Infant Development is used as a comprehensvie behavioral assessment protocol for the infant between 2 and 30 months of age. The standardization of this test was based on the response from a wider, more general population then those of the DDST. The Bayley yields two developmental indices: the mental index and the motor index. Like the DDST, it is not an intelligence test (Nelson 1981). In addition to their clinical uses, these tests have been valuable in research – in assessing, for example, the effects of intervention programs or poor environments.

Promotion of Health

In addition to having a good understanding of prenatal influences, the health professional should be knowledgeable in two additional areas relating to preventing illness and promoting health in infants: immunization and breastfeeding. Immunizations promote resistance to disease through the injection of attenuated, weakened organisms of products produced by organisms (Murray and Zentner 1979). In the United States, infants need the combination of diphtheria and tetanus toxoids and pertussis vaccine (DPT) at prescribed intervals through the first year. At one year or later, the child should receive vaccination for rubeola and rubella. Such vaccinations are essential not only for the well-being of the child, but also to protect other susceptible persons who may have contact with the child.

Because of host-resistant factors in human milk, breast milk offers many advantages to infants (including premature infants) in addition to the psychological benefits of breastfeeding. Human milk contains immunoglobulins and antibodies to many types of microorganisms, especially those found in the intestinal tract, as well as enzymes that destroy bacteria. It is important for all staff members to respect maternal desires, educate women, and establish hospital routines that allow the baby to be with the mother for feeding whenever the infant is hungry and the mother's breasts are full.

The Premature Infant

Although all the factors that contribute to premature birth are not yet known, the research makes it clear that poverty contributes strongly to risk. Poverty is, in fact, a major predictor of unfavorable outcome for children. Another major risk factor is maternal immaturity. Research has shown that adolescents tend to have poor diets; they are more likely to be malnourished while pregnant. A malnourished mother tends to have malnourished children, not only because of her inferior diet but also because of financial problems or lack of information that lead to malnutrition for herself and her children. In addition, an infant born to a malnourished mother is often irritable and difficult to arouse, making feeding interactions stressful and difficult for both the mother and the baby (Reed and Stanley 1977).

Several psychological issues are important in dealing with premature infants. Recent research shows that infants born prematurely are at higher risk for child abuse (Kennell, Voos, and Klaus 1979). The numerous problems of prematurity, which may be minor, are often overwhelming to parents. Diminished parental expectations often result in overprotective behavior that understimulates the infant. The premature infant shows less muscle tone, tires more quickly, has poorly organized sleep patterns, and exhibits poor attentive behavior. However, it is important to assess a premature infant by its gestational age. Premature infants mature at the same rate as full-term infants on most parameters (though their sense of vision matures somewhat faster). Thus, the age of a premature infant must be "corrected" for prematurity through the first 2 years in order to get an accurate assessment (Nelson 1981). This is done by subtracting the number of weeks the infant was born before term from its actual age; a 6-month-old who was 8 weeks premature would be assessed by the standards of development for a 4-month-old.

Interventions by staff can alleviate many of the problems that occur. In one study in which infants were gently rubbed for 5 minutes per hour for 10 days, positive effects were gained immediately and maintained. The stimulated infants were more active and gained weight more quickly than controls. At 7-month follow-up, the experimental group appeared healthier, more active, and more physically capable as demonstrated on tests of motor development (Solkoff et al. 1969). Several studies of low-birth-weight infants and premature infants have demonstrated increased intellectual and sensorimotor development among those children who received sensory stimulation in the nursery and at home compared to controls (Scarr-Salapatek and Williams 1973; Kramer and Pierpont 1976).

Child Abuse

About 6,000 children are killed by their parents or caretakers each year in the United States. Over 600,000 are abused, 60,000 of these cases resulting in significant trauma. In Illinois alone, 62,000 reports of child abuse were made in one year. None of these figures include the full incidence of sexual abuse of which clinicians are becoming increasingly aware (Nelson 1981). Infants less than one year old are at high risk for serious injury or death. Stepchildren and premature or other "defective" children are frequently abused. A recent study found that parents who abused their premature infants had visited them in the intensive-care nursery significantly later after delivery than other parents of premature infants and that the mothers had been significantly more ill during their pregnancies (Kennell, Voos, and Klaus 1979). The characteristics of abusive families are currently being compared, in several large studies, with those of control families on a wide variety of measures. The researchers have noted differences in parent-child interactions. For example, Burgess and Conger (1978) found that members of abusive families interacted less with each other than members of the control families, and when they did interact, they focused more on the negative aspects of their relationships. In another study, Starr (1979) found that abusive mothers spend significantly less time in auditory and tactile stimulation of their infants, were less age-appropriate in their stimulation strategies, and were less tolerant of activities initiated by their infants. Reasons often given by caretakers for abuse support the observations of the Starr study. Most incidents involve problems of feeding, toileting, and comforting to stop crying. Often the small child is gravely injured by a single blow made in frustration (Nelson 1981).

Treatment of abuse has focused on three areas, all involving health professionals: prediction, home visits, and education. Gray et al. (1977) observed mothers during delivery and caring for their newborn. Based on these observations they identified infants at risk for abuse. Half of the risk infants received weekly home visits by medical staff. The characteristics considered predictive of abuse were: social isolation, viewing the upcoming birth as a nuisance or bother, overconcern with the sex of the child, and many anticipated concerns about the problems of routine caretaking. The success of the interventions in this and similar studies have led to proposals for a national health visitor system that would assign a health professional to every mother at risk for abuse and her family from shortly before the birth of a child through the preschool years (Starr 1979). Unfortunately, such a program raises issues of family rights to privacy and brings up the question of the detrimental effects of labeling. A third approach to preventing child abuse is educating prospective parents; there are some educational programs in many junior high and high schools. Research indicates that the key to the elimination of child abuse is primary prevention, an area of potential impact for the health professional.

Grief

The birth of a baby is the culmination of the parents' best efforts and embodies their hopes for the future. Consequently, it is not surprising that the birth of an infant with a congenital abnormality precipitates major family stress. Kennell and colleagues (1979) discussed the stages of reaction that parents go through in adjusting to the infant's special needs. They emphasized that a significant aspect of adaptation is the necessity for parents to mourn the loss of the normal child they had expected. The parents often experience a sequence of identifiable stages of emotional reactions that include shock, disbelief or denial, sadness, anger, anxiety, equilibrium, reorganization. The health professional plays an important role in working with the parents. It has been suggested (Kennell et al. 1979) that the parents be told directly, while they are together and with the baby present, about the problem and possible solutions. Normal, healthy aspects of the infant should be identified. Psychological consultation often helps parents to deal with their wish that the baby would die, their feelings of guilt, their difficulties in forming an attachment to the child, and their overwhelming sense of responsibility. Often the parents' mental picture of the anomaly is far more alarming than the actual handicaps of the infant. Medical staff are often frustrated and upset by the birth of an infant with a congenital anomaly. The temptation to withdraw from the parents and their infant is strong. In their anxiety and grief, parents may be demanding, angry, blaming, or dependent on staff. The health professional can provide emotional support by listening to parents and can demonstrate acceptance of the infant by holding, cuddling, and looking at the infant while talking to the parents.

Parents who relinquish their newborn for adoption are also con-

51

fronted with the crisis of bereavement. Because the decision is often made during the pregnancy, the stages that usually involve attachment and anticipation stimulate ambivalence in parents who give up their child after birth. In addition, the parents must deal with the stresses that have led to their decision to relinquish, such as young maternal age, birth out of wedlock, or lack of family support. Intervention at the prenatal stage can focus on anticipatory grief, anger, depression, decisions about viewing the baby, and choice of post-delivery care. The mother should have an opportunity to view the newborn and have a concrete focus for her grief.

Helping the parents cope with the death of their infant is an important service that health professionals can provide. Some investigators have suggested that the length and intensity of mourning are proportionate to the closeness of the relationship prior to death. It is important that health professionals realize that for some women affectional ties to their babies begin or accelerate with the first fetal movement. Observers have noted intense mourning reactions after a neonatal death, lasting for periods of 4 to 6 months and involving the additional loss of a wish-fulfillment. Grieving patterns are similar in the loss of any loved one: somatic distress, preoccupation with the image of the deceased, guilt, hostile reactions, and loss of the usual patterns of conduct (Klaus and Kennell 1976). The health professional has three major tasks: to help the parents digest the loss and make it real, to ensure that normal grief reactions will begin and that both parents will go through the entire process, and to meet the individual needs of each parent. Parents will be helped in this process if they are allowed to view, touch, and hold their dead infant. Traditional bereavement services should be arranged according to the customs of the family. Staff members often feel a sense of guilt over the death. Culberg (1972) observed three kinds of reactions: avoidance of the situation, projection of feelings onto parents in the form of blaming, and denial. The last coping strategy leads to the common hospital practice of removing all evidence of the baby's existence. This is difficult for parents because nothing remains to confirm the reality of the baby's birth and death. Klaus and Kennell (1976) suggested that the health professional support the parents in their mourning by meeting and discussing feelings right after the death of the child, within the next 2 to 3 days before discharge, and again in 3 to 6 months.

SUMMARY

The infant is more competent, social, and sexual/sensual than observers had previously thought. Most of an infant's capabilities depend on proper physical development. In the past several years, researchers have become more aware of prenatal influences on the infant's physical development. Intervention by medical staff can prevent the negative effects of alcohol, drugs, nicotine, caffeine, infection, and maternal stress. The quality of care that the infant receives from parental figures depends in part on the infant's temperament or particular style in regulating stimuli. Special health issues, such as prematurity or congenital deformities, will also affect the child's relationships with caretakers. Important tasks for health professionals working with this age group involve assessment of normal development, the promotion of immunization and support of breastfeeding, special work with the premature infant and its family, intervention and education to prevent child abuse, and support and guidance for parents who give up a child for adoption, who have an infant with a congenital abnormality, or who have an infant who dies.

REFERENCES

Ainsworth, M.D.S. "Object relations, dependency, and attachment." *Child Development,* 1969, 40:969–1026.

Arnstein, H. "The crisis of becoming a father." *Sexual Behavior,* April 1972, pp. 42–47.

Ball, W., and Tronick, E. "Infant response to impending collision: Optical and real." *Science,* 1971, 171:818–820.

Bell, R. Q. "Stimulus control of parent or caretaker behavior by offspring." *Developmental Psychology,* 1971, 4 (1):63–72.

_____. "Parent, child, and reciprocal influences." *American Psychologist,* 1979, 34:821–826.

Berg, W. K., and Berg, K. M. "Psychophysiological development in infancy: State, sensory function, and attention." In J. D. Osofsky (Ed.), *Handbook of Infant Development.* New York: John Wiley and Sons, 1979.

Bieliauskas, L. A. *Stress and Its Relationship to Health and Illness.* Boulder, Colo.: Westview Press, 1981.

Biller, H. B., and Meredith, D. *Father Power.* New York: David McKay, 1975.

Brackbill, Y. "Obstetrical medication and infant behavior." In J. D. Osofsky

(Ed.), *Handbook of Infant Development*. New York: John Wiley and Sons, 1979.

Brazelton, T. B. "Neonatal behavioral assessment." in T. M. Field, A. M. Sostek, S. Goldberg, and H. H. Shuman (Eds.), *Infants Born at Risk*. New York: Spectrum, 1979.

Brazelton, T. B., Koslowski, B., and Main, M. "The origins of reciprocity: The early mother-infant interaction." In M. Lewis and L. A. Rosenblum (Eds.), *The Effects of the Infant on Its Caretaker*. New York: John Wiley and Sons, 1974.

Bronson, G. "The postnatal growth of visual capacity." *Child Development*, 1974, 45:873–890.

Burgess, R. L., and Conger, R. D. "Family interaction in abusive, neglectful and normal families." *Child Development*, 1978, 49:1163–1173.

Carter, E., and Goldrick, M. *The Family Life Cycle: A Framework for Family Therapy*. New York: Gardner Press, 1980.

Chinn, P. *Child Health Maintenance*. St. Louis: C. V. Mosby and Co., 1974.

Cordero, J. F., Oakley, G. P., Greenberg, F., and James, L. M. "Is Bendectin a teratogen?" *Journal of the American Medical Association*, 1981, 245 (22):2307–2310.

Culberg, J. *Psychosomatic Medicine in Obstetrics and Gynecology*. 3rd International Congress. Basel: S. Karger, 1972.

Davison, A. N., and Dobbing, J. "Myelination as a vulnerable period in brain development." *British Medical Bulletin*, 1966, 22:40–44.

Dennis, W. "Causes of retardation among institutional children." *Journal of Genetic Psychology*, 1960, 96:47–59.

Dott, A., and Fort, A. "The effects of maternal demographic factors on infant mortality rates." *American Journal of Obstetrics and Gynecology*, 1975, 123:847–853.

Drillien, C. M., and Ellis, R.W.B. *The Growth and Development of the Prematurely Born Infant*. Baltimore: Williams and Wilkens, 1964.

Ebbs, J. H., Brown, A., Tisdall, F. F., Moyle, W. J., and Bill, M. "The influence of improved prenatal nutrition upon the infant." *Canadian Medical Association Journal*, 1942, pp. 6–8.

Eichorn, D. H. "Physical development: Current foci of research." in J. D. Osofsky (Ed.), *Handbook of Infant Development*. New York: John Wiley and Sons, 1979.

Erikson, E. H. *Childhood and Society*. 2nd Ed. New York: Norton, 1963.

Escalona, S. *The Roots of Individuality*. Chicago: Aldine Publishing Co., 1968.

––––––. "The differential impact of environmental conditions as a function of different patterns in infancy." In J. C. Westman (Ed.), *Individual Differences in Children*. New York: John Wiley and Sons, 1973.

Fantz, R. L. "Visual experience in infants: Decreased attention to familiar patterns relative to novel ones." *Science*, 1964, 146:668–670.

Feldman, H. S. "Behavior Through the Lifespan: Sexual Development—Infancy Through Aging." Unpublished manuscript, Rush Medical College, Chicago, 1981.

Flanagan, G. L. *The First Nine Months of Life*. New York: Simon and Schuster, 1962.

Freud, A. *The Ego and the Mechanism of Defense*. Translated by C. Baines. New York: International Universities Press, 1948.

Freud, S. *The Ego and the Id*. London: Hogarth, 1950.

Gray, J. D., Cutler, C. A., Dean, J., and Kempe, C. H. "Prediction and prevention of child abuse." *Child Abuse and Neglect*, 1977, 1:45–58.

Greenberg, M., and Morris, N. "Engrossment: The newborn's impact upon the father." *American Journal of Orthopsychiatry*, 1974, 44:520–531.

Guyton, A. *Textbook of Medical Physiology*. 4th Ed. Philadelphia: W. B. Saunders, 1971.

Harlap, S., and Davis, A. "Infant admissions to hospital and maternal smoking." *Lancet*, 1974, 1:529–532.

Hellman, L., and Pritchard, J. *Williams Obstetrics*. 14th Ed. New York: Appleton-Century-Crofts, 1971.

Henderson, J. B., Hall, S. M., and Lipton, H. L. "Changing self-destructive behavior." in G. C. Stone, F. Cohen, and N. E. Adler (Eds.), *Health Psychology*. New York: Jossey-Bass, 1980.

Hill, R. M., Craig, J. P., Chaney, M. D., Tennyson, L. M., and McCulley, L. B. "Utilization of over-the-counter drugs during pregnancy." *Clinical Obstetrics and Gynecology*, 1977, 20:381–394.

Ingelman-Sundberg, A., and Wirsen, C. *A Child is Born*. New York: Dell Publishing, 1965.

Jaeger, W. *The Paideia: The Ideals of Greek Culture*. Vol. 3. New York: Oxford University Press, 1944.

Kaltreider, D. "Patients at high risk for low birth weight delivery." *American Journal of Obstetrics and Gynecology*, 1976, 124:251–256.

Kaplan, B. "Malnutrition and mental deficiency." *Psychological Bulletin*, 1972, 78:321–334.

Kennell, J. H., Voos, D. K., and Klaus, M. H. "Parent-infant bonding." In J. D. Osofsky (Ed.), *Handbook of Infant Development*. New York: John Wiley and Sons, 1979.

Klaus, M. H., and Kennell, J. H. *Maternal-Infant Bonding: The Impact of Early Separation or Loss on Family Development*. St. Louis: C. V. Mosby and Co., 1976.

Kolodny, R. C., Masters, W. H., and Johnson, V. E. *Textbook of Sexual Medicine*. Boston: Little, Brown & Co., 1979.

Kopp, C. B., and Parmelee, A. H. "Prenatal and perinatal influences on infant behavior." In J. D. Osofsky (Ed.), *Handbook of Infant Development*. New York: John Wiley and Sons, 1979.

Kramer, L., and Pierpont, M. "Rocking waterbeds and auditory stimuli to enhance growth of preterm infants." *Journal of Pediatrics,* 1976, 88:297–299.

Landis, C., and Bolles, M. M. *Textbook of Abnormal Psychology.* New York: Macmillan, 1947.

Le Masters, E. "Parenthood as crisis." In H. J. Parad (Ed.), *Crisis Intervention: Selected Readings.* New York: Family Service Association of America, 1971.

Lesser, A. J. "Progress in maternal and child health." *Children Today,* April 1972, pp. 7–12.

Lofgren, K. "Behavior in the Life Cycle: Syllabus for Lectures on the Family." Unpublished manuscript, Rush Medical College, Chicago, 1981.

Longo, L. D. "The biologic effects of carbon monoxide on the pregnant woman, fetus, and new born infant." *American Journal of Obstetrics and Gynecology,* 1977, 129:69–103.

McCauley, C. S. *Pregnancy After 35.* New York: E. P. Dutton and Co., 1978.

Mitchell, A. A., Rosenberg, L., Shapiro, S., and Stone, D. "Birth defects related to Bendectin use in pregnancy." *Journal of the American Medical Association,* 1981, 245 (22):2311–2314.

Moss, H. A., and Robson, K. S. "Maternal influences on early social behavior." *American Journal of Orthopsychiatry,* 1967, 37:394–395.

Murphy, D. P. "The outcome of 625 pregnancies in women subjected to pelvic radium roentgen irradiation." *American Journal of Obstetrics and Gynecology,* 1929, 18:179–187.

_____. *Congenital Malformation.* 2nd Ed. Philadelphia: University of Pennsylvania Press, 1947.

Murphy, L. B. "Coping vulnerability and resilience in childhood." In G. V. Coelho, D. A. Hamburg, and J. E. Adams (Eds.), *Coping and Adaptation.* New York: Basic Books, 1974.

Murray, R. B., and Zentner, J. P. *Nursing Assessment and Health Promotion Through the Life Span.* 2nd Ed. Englewood Cliffs, N.J.: Prentice-Hall, 1979.

Mussen, P. H., Ed. *Carmichael's Manual of Child Psychology.* 3rd Ed. New York: John Wiley and Sons, 1970.

_____. *The Psychological Development of the Child.* 2nd Ed. Englewood Cliffs, N.J.: Prentice-Hall, 1973.

Mussen, P. H., Conger, J. J. and Kagan, J. *Child Development and Personality.* 4th Ed. New York: Harper & Row, 1974.

Mussen, P. H., Conger, J. J., Kagan, J., and Gewitz, J. *Psychological Development: A Life Span Approach.* New York: Harper & Row, 1979.

Nelson, M. N. "Behavior in the Life Cycle: Syllabus for Lectures on Infancy." Unpublished manuscript, Rush Medical College, Chicago, 1981.

Niswander, K. R., and Gordon, M., Eds. *The Collaborative Perinatal Study of the National Institute of Neurological Diseases and Stroke: The Women and Their Pregnancies.* Philadelphia: Saunders, 1972.

Osofsky, J. D., Ed. *Handbook of Infant Development.* New York: John Wiley and Sons, 1979.

Osofsky, J. D., and Connors, K. "Mother-infant interaction: An integrative view of a complex system." In J. D. Osofsky (Ed.), *Handbook of Infant Development.* New York: John Wiley and Sons, 1979.

Pasamanick, B., and Lilienfeld, A. M. "Association of maternal and fetal factors with development of mental deficiency. Part I: Abnormalities in the prenatal and paranatal periods." *Journal of the American Medical Association,* 1955, 159:155–160.

Paul, R. H. "Obstetrics: Basic Equipment Needs." *Clinics in Perinatology,* 1976, 3 (2):361–366.

Phillips, C. R., and Anzalone, J. T. *Fathering: Participation in Labor and Birth.* St. Louis: C. V. Mosby Co., 1978.

Porges, S. W. "Developmental designs for infancy research." In J. D. Osofsky (Ed.), *Handbook of Infant Development.* New York: John Wiley and Sons, 1979.

Ravelli, G. P., Stein, Z. A., and Sussen, M. V. "Obesity in young men after feminine exposure in utero and early infancy." *New England Journal of Medicine,* 1962, 295:349–353.

Reed, D. M., and Stanley, F. J., Eds. *The Epidemiology of Prematurity.* Baltimore: Urban and Schwarzenberg, 1977.

Reese, H. W., and Lipsett, L. P., Eds. *Experimental Child Psychology.* New York: Academic Press, 1970.

Rheingold, H. L. "The modification of social responsiveness in institutional babies." *Monographs of the Society for Research in Child Development,* 1956, 2 (2, Serial No. 63).

Richards, M.P.M. "Obstetric analgesics and the development of children." *Midwife Health Visitor and Community Nurse,* 1976, 12:37–40.

Rosett, H. L., and Sander, L. W. "Effects of maternal drinking on neonatal morphology and state regulation." In J. D. Osofsky (Ed.), *Handbook of Infant Development.* New York: John Wiley and Sons, 1979.

Rothstein, P., and Gould, J. B. "Born with a habit: Infants of drug-addicted mothers." *Pediatric Clinics of North America,* 1974, 21:307–321.

Rudolph, A. M. "Effects of aspirin and acetaminophen in pregnancy and in the newborn." *Archives of Internal Medicine,* 1981, 23:141–143.

Rugh, R., and Shettles, L. *From Conception to Birth: The Drama of Life's Beginnings.* New York: Harper & Row, 1971.

Sameroff, A. J., and Chandler, M. J. "Reproductive risk and the continuum of caretaking casualty." In F. D. Horowitz, M. Hetherington, S. Scarr-Salapatek, and G. Siegel (Eds.), *Review of Child Development Research.* Vol. 4. Chicago: University of Chicago, 1977.

Scarr-Salapatek, S., and Williams, M. "The effects of early stimulation on low-birth-weight infants." *Child Development,* 1973, 44:94–101.

Schaffer, H. R. "Activity level as a constitutional determinant of infantile reaction to deprivation." *Child Development,* 1966, 37:595–602.

Schaffer, H. R., and Emerson, P. "The development of social attachments in infancy." *Monograph of the Society for Research in Child Development,* 29 (3, Whole No. 94), 1964.

Solkoff, N., Yaffe, S., Weintraub, D., and Blase, B. "Effects of handling on the subsequent development of premature infants." *Developmental Psychology,* 1969, 1:765–768.

Sontag, L. W., and Wallace, R. F. "The effect of cigarette smoking during pregnancy upon the fetal heart rate." *American Journal of Obstetrics and Gynecology,* 1935, 29:3–8.

Soyka, L. F. "Effects of Methylxanthines on the fetus." *Clinics in Perinatology,* 1979, 6 (1):37–52.

Starr, R. H. "Child abuse." *American Psychologist,* 1979, 34 (10):872–878.

Thomas, A. "Impact of interest in early individual differences." In H. E. Rie (Ed.), *Perspectives in Child Psychopathology.* Chicago: Aldine Atherton, 1971.

Wainright, W. H. "Fatherhood as a precipitant of mental illness." *American Journal of Psychiatry,* 1966, 123:44.

Westman, J., Ed. *Individual Differences in Children.* New York: John Wiley and Sons, 1973.

Wolman, B. B., and Money, J., Eds. *Handbook of Human Sexuality.* Englewood Cliffs, N.J.: Prentice-Hall, 1980.

EARLY CHILDHOOD DEVELOPMENT

INTRODUCTION

Early childhood is a period of time during which the child becomes more of an individual in the eyes of caretakers and begins to make contact with individuals outside of the family. Compared to the first year, the child's pace of physical growth slows; many bodily activities and physical states are now predictable, routine, and stabilized. Developmental research shifts in emphasis from physical development to cognitive development. Especially interesting are the complex processes of language acquisition and personality development, particularly as they involve interactions with others. During the mother's pregnancy and the first year of the infant's life, the health professional is primarily involved with maintaining and monitoring health. After the first year, the professional may only see the child when there are medical problems, an accident, or infection. Interventions to promote health will often need to be made during these sporadic contacts.

Developmental Tasks

Early childhood spans the years between infancy and elementary school, from 12 months to 5 years. Within early childhood, two other age parameters are occasionally used. Children aged 2 and 3 are often referred to as toddlers; children of 4 and 5 are often called preschoolers. Just as there were significant differences between neonates and infants, the 5-year-old child differs from the 2-year-old. The changes that bring about these differences occur in an orderly sequence and according to the basic principles of development.

59

During this age period, the child is primarily concerned with the following tasks:

1. Settling into orderly daily routines.
2. Mastering toilet training and other self-maintenance tasks.
3. Becoming a family member and gradually increasing participation within the family.
4. Learning to communicate effectively with an increasing number of other people.
5. Conforming to the expectations of others; becoming socialized.
6. Developing the ability to handle potentially dangerous situations.

THE FAMILY

As children become capable of greater independent exploration and language acquisition, they begin to behave as individuals within the family. This causes important changes for all the family members. If the caretaker has been comfortable with a dependent baby, the independence of the toddler may be threatening. Conversely, some people who have difficulty caring for a dependent infant feel more creative and loving to a child "they can talk to." The parents need to revise their practices to complement the child's emerging independence without jeopardizing safety. Finding a balance between permitting free expression and simultaneously setting limits is often difficult. Unfortunately, parental figures may find themselves being punitive as a primary means of controlling the behavior of the child. Several learning theorists have systematized methods for setting limits that tend to be more effective than punishment alone. Among those that are helpful for this age group are:

1. Reward (reinforce) appropriate behavior through approval and attention. Negative attention, such as yelling, is more appealing to the child than no attention. Consequently, the child whose appropriate behavior is ignored but whose inappropriate behavior is acknowledged through scolding will continue to misbehave (Skinner 1957). Reinforcement increases the likelihood of a behavior occurring again.
2. When limits are set, explain what the child is doing wrong,

what the consequences of the behavior would be (to teach cause and effect), and what behavior can be performed instead. Say, for example, "Don't touch the vase, it might fall off. Play with your toy instead" (Patterson 1975; 1976).

3. Reward and set limits consistently so the child will begin to internalize the rules and not test the adult's endurance in each situation (Patterson 1975).

4. Set limits only when necessary so that child does not become confused and overly self-conscious (Patterson 1976).

5. If possible, provide a space that is identified as an area of maximum freedom.

6. As the child gets older, allow discussion and negotiation of family rules with the parental figures having the final say (Kagan 1979).

Parenting Styles

Several attempts have been made within the developmental research to ascertain the most positive family style that produces the healthiest children (for example, Baumruid 1967; Murray and Zentner 1979). There are, however, various limitations to a simplistic attitude toward parenting skills. First, there is reason to question the premise that universal behavioral outcomes can be expected to result from particular styles of child rearing. For example, investigators observed 2½-year-olds who were raised according to two very different parenting styles; some children received care from their mothers while others spent half of their waking hours in a supportive day-care center. All the children were found to be alike on indices of degree of attachment, attentiveness, language proficiency, and vulnerability to anxiety (Kagan, Kearsley, and Zelazo 1978). In other studies, similar parental behaviors led to different outcomes for boys and girls (Baumruid 1967; Kagan and Moss 1972; Moss and Robson 1968). Second, the premise that some universally successful parenting style exists does not take into account observed temperamental differences in children at very early ages (Westman 1973). The same style of parenting—for example, setting high achievement goals—could be encouraging to growth in one child and overwhelming to another. Longitudinal studies on parenting frequently found that adaptive behavior at one age may not be effective at another (Kagan 1979). In addition, research has suggested that global factors such as cultural or ethnic background have stronger influences than parenting styles (Kagan, Kearsley, and Zelazo 1978; Kagan, Lapidus, and Moore 1978).

This is not to say that parental behaviors do not influence the child, but rather that they influence the child in complex ways. Parental behaviors influence within the context of the child's temperament, the cultural setting, and the age of child. Rather than expecting to obtain universal results for a certain style, it may be more profitable to take a more focused view. Certain parental behaviors and experiences could be viewed in relation to specific traits in children: for example, increased achievement among females (Billingham 1978; Reese and Palmer 1970), aggressiveness in males (Schwarz 1979), or accelerated cognitive development (Yarrow, Rubenstein and Pederson 1975). Consequently, this discussion of parental influences will focus on advantages and disadvantages of particular parental actions upon different aspects of development.

Maternal Employment Outside the Home

Presently, almost 42 percent of mothers of preschoolers are employed outside the home. Among the group whose employment rate has been the lowest (women who live with their husbands, and have children under 3) more than one-third are now employed. Employment rates are also higher for mothers in single-parent families, and the number of single-parent families is also increasing (Hoffman 1979). Consequently, the effects of maternal employment outside the home and how they relate to the issues of single-parent families is important when considering early childhood development.

In the last 30 years, family size in this country has decreased, and household operations have become more efficient. Therefore, it is possible that time spent working outside the home simply fills the time previously consumed by greater household burdens and more children (Hoffman 1979). Several studies have examined the consequences of mothers working outside the home in terms of adjustments in their life-styles and relationships with their children. First, working mothers generally do not put their young children in institutions. In fact, most preschool children of women who work outside the home are cared for in their own homes rather than in day-care centers. Furthermore, studies have thus far not found any adverse effects of quality day care for young children (Belsky and Sternberg 1978; Kagan 1979), or problems with multiple attachments (Ainsworth 1967; Lamb 1979). In a study of middle-class preschoolers, there was no difference in the amount of one-to-one mother-child contact for working and nonworking mothers (Goldberg 1977). In recent research (Gold and Andres 1978; Gold, Andres, and Glorieux 1979), 4-year-olds whose mothers had worked since birth were compared with 4-year-olds whose mothers had not worked outside the home. No adverse effects were found except that the sons of working mothers had lower IQ scores. This is consistent with previous research that found that daughters of employed mothers performed better on achievement tests while sons did not perform as well (Hoffman 1974). The effects of maternal employment following divorce depended on how disruptive the divorce proved to be. Hetherington (1979), studying 4-year-olds, found that if the mother was employed prior to divorce the job helped her cope more effectively, both psychologically and economically. But if the mother started her employment at the time of the divorce, although employment enhanced her self-esteem, the child had more difficulty because the home routine was disrupted.

Effects of Divorce

How divorce affects children depends on the same developmental factors that influence other changes. Temperamentally difficult children have been found to be less adaptable to change and more vulnerable to adversity than are temperamentally easy children (Chess, Thomas, and Birch 1968; Hetherington 1979). Such children will have more difficulty adjusting to divorce and may be more susceptible to long-term effects. Because of limits in cognitive development, the young child is likely to misinterpret the cause of the divorce and blame himself. Children often have grossly distorted perceptions of the parents' emotions, needs, and behavior, as well as of the prospects of reconciliation or total abandonment (Hetherington 1979; Tessman 1978; Wallerstein and Kelly 1975). Factors relating to divorce that affect children of all ages have important influences on the young child. These factors include the degree of conflict (Hetherington 1972), the degree of father absence (Hetherington, Cox, and Cox 1978), and the extent to which economic and daily life are disrupted (Marsden 1969).

By understanding how development in early childhood relates to family issues, the health professional may take an active role in educating parents. Both parents and staff working with this age group need to develop skills in modifying and setting limits on the behaviors of young children. Hospitalization can be especially disruptive at this stage of development, when the child and family are attempting to establish routine and stabilize the tasks of daily maintenance. Hospital staff should know that adherence to as much routine as possible may facilitate coping for the preschool child. In addition, because children of this age are beginning to deal with separation from parents, hospitalization may result in regressive behavior stemming from separation anxiety, particularly for children who have recently experienced disruption resulting from divorce or maternal employment.

PHYSICAL DEVELOPMENT

The rate of growth in the early childhood years is slower than in infancy but follows the same general principles of orderliness, discontinuity, differentiation, cephalocaudal development, and proximodistal and bilateral development. Illness and periods of malnutrition can temporarily slow a child's rate of growth, but when diseases are cured or missing nutrients are supplied, a catch-up phenomenon usually occurs. However, in cases of long-term illness or deprivation, if actual damage to internal organs results, full compensation may never occur.

Growth

The average 2-year-old in the United States stands approximately 81 to 84 cm high (32–33 inches) and weighs about 11 to 13 kg (26–28 pounds). By age 5, height has increased to 109 to 111 cm (43–44 inches) and weight from 18 to 19 kg (39–41 pounds) (Freiberg 1979). Arms and legs grow the fastest during early childhood; head growth is much slower. Head circumference has already reached 68 percent of adult size by age 2, 70 percent of adult size by age 5. This growth causes a change in proportions; no longer the chubby, top-heavy infant, the child now more nearly resembles an adult.

By age 2, respirations average 25 per minute, and this remains so through the age of 5 (Murray and Zentner 1979). Lung volume has increased; and susceptibility to respiratory infection is less than in infancy. In the circulatory system, the pulse decreases; the 5-year-old's pulse rate is normally 80 to 110 and blood pressure is about 90/60, systolic and diastolic. Body temperature averages 99°F (37.2°C) (Chinn 1974). Visual acuity and the ability to accommodate (visually adjust to objects at varying distances) continue to develop. At age 2, vision is 20/10; by age 5 vision is 20/50 to 20/30. Visual acuity becomes important in the process of developing eye-hand coordination.

Neuromuscular skills emerge, are practiced, and are refined as the child ages. Freiberg (1979, p. 141) presents a rich picture of the comparison of abilities for toddlers and preschoolers:

> At age two, children walk upstairs holding onto a hand, rail, or wall. They place both feet on each step before proceeding to the next. By age three they begin to alternate their feet, one to a step. By age four they have usually ceased to hold on to anything and alternate steps going both down and up. By age five they may well run up the stairs. For many two-year-olds holding a glass of liquid and drinking without spilling is a feat. By age three children can drink well and feed themselves complete meals with very little assistance. At age three, children undress (quite successfully) and attempt to dress (less successfully). By age five, children dress without assistance, including washing faces, hands, and brushing teeth. Five-year-olds may even be able to tie the laces of their shoes in neat bows. Three-year-olds learn to jump over or off objects and maintain their balance. Five-year-olds learn to jump rope in rhythm.

These increases in skills are due to neuromuscular maturation and repetition of movements. The motor cortex and pyramid tracts (tracts running from the motor area of the cerebral cortex and descending down the spinal cord) are more mature, intricate, and efficient. Myelinization, or the acquiring of a protective sheath (myelin sheath) around nerve fibers, becomes complete enough to support most movement. Cortical and subcortical regions of the brain have matured so that sleep, wakefulness, and emotional responses become better regulated, allowing for greater capacity to learn new motor skills.

The black child becomes more advanced developmentally than the white child during this period. By age 2, the black child is taller, heavier, and has more advanced skeletal development and less subcutaneous fat. Dentition is also more advanced in black children if variables for nutrition are the same (Murray and Zentner 1979).

COGNITIVE DEVELOPMENT

Cognitive development is of great importance at this stage. It allows the child a more complex means of communication, the ability to participate in symbolic play, and more sophisticated problem-solving skills. Cognitive abilities should be understood by the health professional who needs to determine how the child will conceptualize illness and death.

Piaget

The second broad period of intellectual development according to Piaget is the preoperational, extending from approximately 18 months to 7 years of age. Recall that at the end of the first period of cognitive development, the sensorimotor, the infant manipulates objects and uses them to attain goals. In the sensorimotor stage, all thinking and reasoning is limited to objects and events that are immediately present and directly perceived (Mussen 1973). In contrast, in the the preoperational period the child begins to use mental symbols—images or words—that represent objects that are not present. For example, a bike may be an imagined airplane, or a piece of cloth might become a dress. A child's ability to imitate parental figures who are not present also illustrates the use of symbols. The preoperational child clearly demonstrates the ability to remember people or things that move out of sight. The capacity to recall and remember something out of sight is described by Piaget as object constancy and implies that the child has formed an internal representation of the object (Gordon 1981).

During the early part of the preoperational stage, between the ages of approximately 2 and 4, children are egocentric; that is, centered around themselves (Mussen 1973). The young child is unable to take another person's point of view. This is clearly seen in speech and communication: Little real effort is made to adapt what the child says to the needs of the listener. Gordon (1981, p. 3) describes an example of such egocentric thinking: "Suppose, for example, you hold a playing card between yourself and a young boy so that he sees the ace of diamonds and you see the back. If you ask him to describe what you are seeing, he most likely will describe the ace of diamonds. He describes what he sees because he tends to think that everyone sees, feels, and thinks as he does." The thinking of children this age also has magical and animistic elements. For example, the child is apt to feel that "clouds move because they don't like to be so close to the sun." Objects are treated as living and motivated to do things. There is little notion of accident or coincidence. The child at the preoperational stage, unlike the older child, usually is not concerned with a sophisticated understanding of cause and effect relationships. Young children tend to justify events rather than explain their causes.

Preoperational children, up to approximately 5 years of age, are unable to abstract by use of classification. If asked to sort various geometric shapes according to shape, they cannot; the sort will be either random or done according to color. From 5 to 7 years old, the child begins to be able to reason on the basis of size, shape, and color concepts but is limited in the ability to abstract. The child cannot reason simultaneously about a whole and a part of the whole. Consequently, a red flower is classified as either "red" or "flower" but not both (Gordon 1981). The child is also unable to seriate – position sticks according to increase in size. Concepts at this stage are a function of the child's immediate judgment and perceptions, and an object or event is perceived according to only a single salient aspect.

Piaget's conceptualization of children's cognitive abilities in the preoperational stage has been helpful as a basis for evaluating children. His research has been criticized, however, for being inaccurate regarding age (Flavell 1977). Many children are capable of performing tasks at an age younger than Piaget would project. The sequence of mastery of tasks remains constant. Children who are hospitalized and under stress will often perform more poorly on cognitive tasks than when they are under less stressful conditions (Gordon 1981).

Conceptualizations of Illness

Researchers have investigated the causal thinking of children in diverse areas: sex and birth (Bernstein and Cowan 1975; Kreitler and Kreitler 1966; Nagy 1953a), internal body functioning (Gellert 1962; Nagy 1953b), and medical procedures (Steward and Regalbuto 1975). In addition, a number of studies have examined children's conceptions of health and illness (Brodie 1974; Campbell 1975; Mechanic 1964). Campbell found that younger children were likely to talk about feeling ill in terms of vague, nonlocalized feelings, whereas older children gave relatively more attention to specific diseases or diagnoses. Palmer and Lewis (1975, p. 2) found that young children attributed illness to such causes as "going out without a jacket and eating too much candy." Older children, however, were more likely to list "contact with ill people and germs" as causes of illness.

Bibace and Walsh (1980) recently conducted a large study that used Piaget's framework and which explored children's conceptualizations of health and illness. Such a framework allows the health professional to assess a child's understanding of illness and to present information about procedures as clearly as possible. Bibace and Walsh found clear parallels between the ways in which children understand illness and the cognitive processes of the preoperational child as described by Piaget. When a young child discusses illness, issues of causality are unclear. The child either evades questions of cause or gives magical causes: "A heart attack is from the sun." How does the sun cause a heart attack? "It's the sun, that's all!" (Bibace and Walsh 1980, p. 291). Children also center on just one aspect of illness, another characteristic described by Piaget. A child this age will link something like "going to the hospital" with illness and will perseverate on this concept and not attend to issues of pain or taking medicine. Bibace and Walsh (1980, p. 291) explain the concept of contagion for children this age:

> Illness is defined in terms of a single external symptom, such as a physical activity, that is usually observed in connection with the illness and is often restricted inappropriately to a single body part. The source of the illness is usually either a person or object that is spatially near to, but not touching, the ill person, or an activity or event that is temporally prior to, but not simultaneous with, the occurrence of the illness. Significant at this level is the child's inability to articulate the causal link between the source of the illness and the illness itself. When asked how an illness is contracted, the child merely reasserts the spatial or temporal proximity, often invoking or implying some form of the general process of contagion. Similarly, the source of the cure is usually perceived as a person or object in the immediate environment, or an event or activity that occurs subsequent to the illness.

Knowledge of these conceptualizations has practical application when working with children this age. Taking into account a developmental analysis of the patient's conception of illness may render understandable fears that the adult might consider irrational. For example, many 5- and 6-year-old children on a hospital pediatric ward became unexpectedly upset and wanted to move to another room. Their fear was based on their preoccupation with catching the disease of their roommate (contagion) (Bibace and Walsh 1980). In another case a younger child was afraid that a stethoscope was used to find out "if I have a heart" (Bibace and Walsh 1980, p. 300). In such cases, the health professional can reassure both the caretaker and the child by recognizing that such concerns are normal for young children and should not be dismissed.

Conceptualizations of Death

Similar to Bibace and Wallace's work on conceptualizations of illness among children is Nagy's (1959) work involving children's understanding of death. Using open-ended techniques, such as compositions, drawings, and discussions, Nagy studied the ways in which 3- to 10-year-olds view death. She identified three stages in the conceptualization of death that parallel normal intellectual development. The first stage occurs from ages 3 to 5. Children in this age group deny death as a final irrevocable process. They feel that death is temporary. Many feel that a dead person is the same as a live one but living under different circumstances or in a different place. This is because, as Piaget noted, children of this age do not have a good sense of time; the concept of forever is meaningless to them. These children do not have a clear sense of what is alive and what is not alive. They believe clouds are alive because they move and don't understand the concept of nonlife. A preschooler's lack of understanding of the permanence of death may be upsetting to a recently widowed spouse because the child may frequently ask where the deceased parent is. For children of this age group, the most painful aspect is the immediate separation imposed by the death rather than death itself (Nagy 1959). The health professional's role in dealing with these issues will be explained in the section on health considerations.

Language Acquisition

Among the most important cognitive tasks the young child achieves is the acquisition of language. Language is a structured symbolic system for communication consisting of two major aspects: (1) structure, or basic units and rules for arranging them; and (2) meaning or semantics (Brocken 1981). Since the late 1950s the field of psycholinguistics—the psychological study of language and its development—has become very prominent and productive. Large samples of children's vocalizations and speech have been recorded and minutely analyzed. Although the process of language is not yet fully understood, it is clear that children's language has definite, structural properties.

The normal child begins to speak by 15 months, although some children may make little effort to speak until after 2 years. If a child is delayed in speaking there may be a problem in receptive language development (understanding of language) or expressive language development (articulating representation in words of a language) or both. Tables 3-1 and 3-2 describe the average behaviors observed that demonstrate both aspects of language acquisition for normal children. The items in parentheses indicate the need for a hearing, speech, or language evaluation (Brocken 1981).

Recognizable language develops sequentially. First the child uses nouns of one syllable in syncretic speech (in which a single word represents an entire sentence). Then children use single verbs to connote action. By age 2, the child uses telegraphic speech. This consists of two- to four-word expressions that contain a noun and verb and maintain word order, such as "go Daddy." Adjectives, then adverbs, and then other grammatical components are learned from 18 months on. As the child becomes more experienced, variety of intonation also increases. The last area of language development is the use of pronouns. By age 3, the child has a vocabulary of hundreds of words (Brocken 1981). The speech of 4-year-old children reveals that they have mastered most of the important grammatical rules governing word order, the formation of plurals, and the past and future tenses.

One of the major issues in language development is the extent to which language acquisition represents an innate or environmentally determined process. Clearly environmental influences are strong: A child cannot acquire a label or concept of something that is not part of the culture; if others speak indistinctly to the child, the child will also speak indistinctly; and the parents teach rules and meanings by expanding the shortened sentences expressed by the child. On the other hand, the most impressive arguments about the overriding importance of maturation concern the amazingly rapid development of

TABLE 3-1
EXPRESSIVE LANGUAGE DEVELOPMENT

AGE	OBSERVED BEHAVIOR
6 mos. - 1 yr.	Babbling changes to vocal play; imitates sounds.
1 - 1½ yrs.	Vocabulary size: 10 - 100 words. Jargon is used purposefully
1½ - 2 yrs.	Vocabulary size: 100 - 200 words. Puts 2 words together, "Go bye-bye." Refers to himself by name. Says or sings short rhymes. (2 yrs. If child hasn't said first word; if jargon persists; if child began talking and then stopped -- evaluate.)
2 - 2½ yrs.	Vocabulary size: 200 - 400 words. Uses 2 word sentences. Uses future tense, some plurals.
2½ - 3 yrs.	Vocabulary size: 400 - 850 words. Gives full name. Uses past tense. (3 yrs. If child is not using at least 2 word combinations -- evaluate.)
3 - 4 yrs.	Vocabulary size: 850 - 1500 words. Uses 3 word sentences. Speech 90% intelligible. Relates experience. (4 yrs. If speech is largely unintelligible -- evaluate.)
4 - 5 yrs.	Vocabulary size: 1500 - 2000 words. Uses 4 word sentences. Uses compound and complex sentences. Grammar approximates grammatical patterns of adults. Can relate a long story accurately. (5 yrs. If sentence structure is noticeably faulty -- evaluate.)
5 - 6 yrs.	Vocabulary size: 2000 - 2500 words. Uses 5 word sentences. Uses all prepositions and conjunctions appropriately.

Source: Brocken (1981).

TABLE 3-2
RECEPTIVE LANGUAGE DEVELOPMENT

AGE	OBSERVED BEHAVIOR
6 mos. - 1 yr.	Locates sound source. Responds differently to different sounds. Understands some words, e.g., comes when called; obeys "no"; identifies some objects when named.
1 - 1½ yrs.	Attends to sounds in another room. Points to body parts when named. Understands simple sentences.
1½ - 2 yrs.	Obeys simple commands. Shows interest in TV commercials.
2 - 2½ yrs.	Listens to brief picture stories. Responds to different forms of personal pronouns.
2½ - 3 yrs.	Locates sound in another room. Listens to stories or TV for 15-20 minutes. Understands direct vs. indirect objects; negative forms.
3 - 4 yrs.	Carries out 2 commands.
4 - 5 yrs.	Carries out 3 commands. Understands tenses; plural vs. singular. Acquires information from children's program.
5 - 6 yrs.	Begins simple classifications. Acquires information from spoken language of life- situation TV programs.

SOURCE: Brocken (1981).

the child's comprehension and use of language, particularly early mastery of grammar. While no real language appears before 18 months of age, children master even complex rules of grammar by about 3½ or 4 years of age—a short span of 24 months (Mussen 1973).

The Relationship of Language and Thought

Language is involved in almost all cognition—thinking, abstraction, concept formation, planning, reasoning, remembering, judging, and solving problems. It is logical that the child's cognitive abilities progress markedly as language is acquired and verbal competence improves. However, although language development facilitates complex cognitive functioning – it should not be inferred that thinking or reasoning is impossible without language. Deaf children are only slightly handicapped in many intellectual and cognitive tasks, including tests of reasoning, even though they are considerably retarded in verbal ability.

In relation to cognitive development for this age group, health professionals have three concerns. First, they must make decisions for referral to evaluate possible cognitive, speech, hearing, or language deficits. Second, by understanding the cognitive capabilities of the child, the health professional may modify health-management practices to respect these limitations. Third, the health professional may use this knowledge to educate parents in relating more effectively with their children.

SEXUAL DEVELOPMENT

For the young child, sexual development involves two processes: first, an increase in body awareness and second, the development of gender identity and sex-role identification.

At 2 years of age, children begin to articulate sexual awareness. They name genitals, distinguish boys from girls, and differentiate the genders of adults ("Mom is a lady"). They are interested in their own bodies and the bodies of others. This is also the first time children are able to refer to themselves by name – an important factor in the beginning of the process of body image, sexual identity, and self-concept. At 2½ years, children differentiate male and female roles even further (Wolman and Money 1980). They are aware of their own genders and how they are like or different from parents. They can see, for example, how boys and fathers have similar genitalia or that both stand to urinate (Feldman 1981). At this age, children show increased interest in the physiological differences of the sexes as well as increased consciousness of their own sex organs. It is not uncommon for children of this age to handle their genitals when dressing or ask their mothers about the functions of breasts. Since gender distinctions are more obvious to others, the socialization process into male and female identities and roles continues with greater intensity. Toys given as gifts, kind of clothing, color of clothing and room, and behavior toward and expectations of the child teach and reinforce society's concept of gender. In conjunction with their emerging sexual consciousness, children imitate and observe parental figures of their own and the opposite sex.

By approximately 3 years of age, a marked intensification of sexual interest and capacity for erotic responses occurs. Both males and females achieve sexual pleasure through self-stimulation, and although girls masturbate less than boys (Murray and Zentner 1979), both exhibit an increase in handling of their genitals. Children also initiate more attachment behaviors through cuddling, kissing, touching, and hugging caretakers and other people important to them (Kolodny, Masters, and Johnson 1979). By age 4 children have no difficulty stating their own genders (Mussen et al. 1979). The 4-year-old child is capable of a great deal more independent movement and is usually involved with other children. This often leads to both homosexual and heterosexual play and experimentation (Wolman and Money 1980). The 4-year-old, with increased cognitive abilities, shows greater interest in sexual questions such as "Where do babies come from?" (Feldman 1981). In response to an increase in body awareness, the child carefully maintains his or her own privacy, although showing a great deal of interest in the bathroom behavior of others (Wolman and Money 1980).

The 5-year-old exhibits a shift in behavior. The child at this age becomes somewhat more modest, sex plays and games of show decrease, and there is less bathroom play and interest in bathroom behavior (Feldman 1981). Children become more involved in imitating adult roles. They often are interested in babies and pregnancy and act this out in play. At the age of 5, boys become more persistent than girls in establishing exclusive sex-typed roles during play (Hetherington and Parke 1975).

Familial Factors in Sex-Role Development

Several general theories of sex-role development have been proposed. Freud believed that sex-role identification with parental figures is central to all personality development during childhood. David Lynn (1974) proposed a theory that focuses on sex-role identification as an important, but not all-encompassing, aspect of personality development. His hypothesis is that in our culture, where lack of early father contact with children is common, both male and female infants initially identify with the mother. As the child ages, males must switch their identification to a masculine role that is taught both by mothers and fathers. Females have the mother, or a female caretaker, frequently present to directly model the feminine role. Males, however, have briefer exposure to male models and must learn by negative example not to be feminine. Several early studies support this theory. Hartley and colleagues (1962) found that sex-role behaviors for boys were seldom defined positively as something the child should do, but rather that boys were punished for what they should not do. Lansky (1968) found that both mothers and fathers of preschool children responded more negatively to opposite-sex choices in toys and activities by boys than they did to opposite-sex choices by girls. Hartup and Zook (1960), in a longitudinal study, found that boys have an earlier and sharper awareness of sex-appropriate behaviors and interests. Girls are more variable and show strong preferences for masculine games and activities. More recent research indicates that females are changing more in accordance with recent cultural changes than are males. In a study of nursery-school children, girls were likely to play with a wide variety of toys and act out careers that have typically been held by either men or women. Little boys, however, were still rigid in picking sex-stereotyped toys and making female/male distinctions in assigning careers. The boys behaved this way whether or not their mothers had careers in male-dominated fields (Billingham 1978).

Health professionals often find themselves being questioned by parents about the normalcy of the sexual behavior of their children. Parents also often ask how to explain sex to their children. In such cases, the cultural, religious, and family values need to be assessed as well as the developmental stage of the child. In addition, caretakers should understand that explanations should be appropriate to the child's level of cognitive development.

PERSONALITY DEVELOPMENT

Personality is a broad and comprehensive concept that refers to the organization of an individual's predispositions and unique adjustments to an environment. Personal characteristics or traits, emotions, motivations, values, goals, and ways of perceiving are all aspects of personality structure (Mussen 1973). The groundwork for personality development begins with the interaction of an infant's temperament and personal environment. During early childhood, specific aspects of personality begin to become apparent. I will review the stages of personality development presented by Freud and Erikson and go on to explore the creation of friendships outside the family.

Freud

According to Freud, the second stage of development, the anal stage, occurs when the child is a toddler. During this stage, children first learn that they can control social interactions, make choices, and deny their parents' wishes. Toilet training is a major developmental accomplishment for this stage. Freud viewed toilet training as psychologically complex. Fears, goals, and conflicting wishes arise. Caretakers give approval not only for defecating properly, but also for withholding feces. The sensations of giving and withholding feces, imitation of parents and siblings, approval from family, and pride in accomplishments are all involved. Often parents become anxious, threatening, and overemphasize the aesthetic and cultural connotations of feces being "dirty" and "smelly." According to Freud, such attitudes generalize to feelings about self, issues of neatness and approval, and increased power struggles.

The next stage of development from a Freudian perspective occurs during the preschool years. During this time the child develops a sexual identification. This involves the well-known oedipal complex – the child becomes attached to the parent of the opposite sex and competitive with the parent of the same sex. Often the child demonstrates this attachment by desiring to spend time and participate in activities exclusively with one parent. When the parent of the same sex sets limits and reconfirms the marital relationship, the child resolves conflicting feelings by identifying with that parent in hopes of someday obtaining the love object (a man like father or a woman like mother). Critics of Freud have been strongest in debating his views of how females resolve this conflict. According to Freud, the female accepts the "inadequacy" of her body, known as penis envy, and, at best, remains neurotic throughout life. Research has challenged these assumptions: Girls of this age do not report "having something missing." In fact, some little boys report jealousy over not being able to have a baby "like Mommy does" (Sherman 1975).

Erikson takes a broader view of the tasks of personality development in early childhood. According to his theory, the toddler is involved in the conflict of autonomy versus shame and doubt. Freud saw self-control of the sphincter muscles and in motor abilities as important developmental accomplishments. Erikson's concept of autonomy includes these abilities but also involves other areas of self-control. Children learn that they can adequately cope with problems or get necessary help; they learn to wait with patience, to give generously or to hold on when that is appropriate, to distinguish between self and others, and to have a sense of good will and pride (Erikson 1963). Shame and doubt develop if autonomy and its resultant positive self-concept are not achieved. Shame, according to Erikson, is the feeling of being fooled, embarrassed, exposed, small, impotent, dirty, and full of rage against self. Doubt is fear, uncertainty, mistrust, lack of self-confidence, and feeling that nothing done is any good; the child feels controlled by others rather than being in control of self (Erikson 1963). The views of Freud and Erikson make clear how the issues of increased competence and independence of the child, as well as problems the family may have in establishing routines of daily care, may have either overall negative or positive effects on the developing self-concept of the toddler.

Erikson's delineation of the next stage recognizes the increased mobility and contact of the preschooler with others outside the family. Erikson defines the period from ages 3 to 6 as that of initiative versus guilt. This is the time when children face the major issues of development of sexual identity, superego development, and peer relationships. Children learn to undertake, plan, and reflect on their behavior. They may experience guilt over real or fantasized events either as a result of real, external punishment or an internal, imagined guilt. Values, judgments, and attitudes are incorporated from three sources: family, peers, and other adult authorities such as teachers and caretakers.

Friendships and Play

Many interpretations have been made of the function and meaning of play. The psychoanalytic view is that play is a symbolic expression of both wishes and defensive actions. Erikson recognized the role of play in helping children become socialized: Children learn the rules of fair play, to share, to help, and to be helped. It is clear that from infancy play activities allow the child to exercise, learn to manage body parts, improve muscular coordination and manual dexterity, and develop spatial and sensory perception. All observers would agree that play is a pleasurable spontaneous activity in which the child is physically active.

As the child develops cognitively and physically, play behavior develops as well. Play behavior also expresses emerging sexual identity. As a means for socialization, play behavior follows a sequence. The toddler tends to engage in parallel play—two children will play independently with different toys within proximity of each other. Interactions between toddlers of the same age tend to be conflictual or initiated and facilitated by adults. The correlation between chronological age and social participation is substantial (Murray and Zentner 1979). By preschool age, children identify somewhat with a play group. They follow rules, become aware of the status of self compared with others, develop perceptions of social relationships, begin the capacity for self-criticism, and state traits and characteristics of others that are admirable or disliked (Murray and Zentner 1979). The preschool play group differs from later ones in that it is loosely organized. The activities of the group may be continuous but membership changes frequently as children join or leave the group at will. Rivalry among children appears as early as age 3 or 4. Rivalry usually involves jealousy of the attention another child is receiving from an adult. Competition, which means trying to improve one's own performance in direct comparison to someone else's performance, does not appear until the child is older. Grabbing toys and disrupting another's play activity, which may be viewed by adults as competitive, is more a reflection of the child's intrusive manner, short attention span, and lack of social skills.

The role of the health professional in personality development of the young child may be diverse and indirect. For example, parents may ask for guidance in parenting skills; young children will demonstrate special needs for mastery and independence on pediatric units; and a nursery school or day-care center may require health consultation. An overview of the relevant health issues for young children may provide a framework for specific interventions.

HEALTH CARE CONSIDERATIONS

Common health problems in early childhood are respiratory infections and accidents. Most frequent are accidents in motor vehicles, burns, drowning, falls, and poisoning. Accidents are the leading cause of death, and death from poisoning continues to increase. Congenital abnormalities are the second leading cause of death (Murray and Zentner 1979). Considering these data, safety promotion is clearly of primary importance for this age group. In addition, the health profesional should be aware of nutritional needs, the need for immunization, and problems parents have complying with medical regimens. The professional should know how to prepare children for hospitalization and be familiar with the issues involving terminally ill children.

Safety Promotion

The first step of safety promotion is child-proofing the home. This can involve the following steps:

1. Cover sharp corners of furniture, steps, counters, etc.
2. Put safety plugs in outlets; block access to heating equipment and hot water.
3. Place poisons, cleaning fluids, weapons, medicines, and sharp knives and tools in high, locked cabinets.
4. Place gates at tops of stairways and screens on windows.
5. Put safety catches on doors and cabinets.
6. Be consistent in defining safe and unsafe areas to play.
7. Place favorite toys and objects on low shelves and within a child's reach.

Protecting the firstborn is less complex because dangerous objects may be put away and more time is available for supervision. However, when there are a number of children in the home, the activities and toys of older siblings may be dangerous for the younger children. As the children grow older, they become more capable of learning clear-cut safety rules and engaging in self-protective behavior that can be reinforced.

Nutritional Needs

Adequate nutrition consists of a diet balanced with proteins, carbohydrates, and fats plus sufficient vitamins and minerals. It can be achieved by giving children two or more servings every day from each of the four basic food groups: milk; vegetables and fruits; meat, fish, and poultry; and breads and cereals. Unfortunately, a well-balanced diet may be difficult to attain. Appetites decrease and fluctuate from day to day, mealtime often becomes a time to test independence by refusing food, and children discover junk food. Because young children burn up their intake of mealtime calories rapidly, snacks of substantive nutritive value should be provided.

Immunization

Routine medical examinations on an annual basis during early childhood serve multiple purposes. Booster shots for immunization received in infancy are necessary. Children must also be carefully assessed for infections and other disease conditions because they lack the cognitive, language, and self-awareness capacities to describe discomforts. Regular check-ups may also reveal problems that may be hidden from caretakers. Among these are: developmental delays, visual or hearing defects, heart murmurs, iron-deficiency anemia, unsuspected urinary tract infection, perceptual problems, neurological dysfunctions, and many other conditions that might otherwise remain undetected until the child enters school (Freiberg 1979). Early detection often increases the success of interventions and reduces the severity of disorders.

Health professionals are becoming increasingly aware of compliance issues and effects on treatment outcome. Actual estimates have recently been as high as 80 percent noncompliance (Goldsmith 1966). Methods that may be used to increase compliance are: educating caretakers regarding the rationale for the treatment regimen, altering the regimens to fit the daily family routine, and building in frequent recordings of results and social reinforcement (acknowledgment) to caretakers for following medical treatments.

Preparation for Hospitalization

Health professionals should understand that young children have special needs in relation to hospitalization. They must be sensitive in dealing with children's concerns with separation as well as their limits in cognitive understanding of procedures. Care should be taken to provide a predictable routine and to allow the child extensive contact with caretakers. In addition, research has indicated that effective preparation for hospitalization for this age group leads to improved recovery (Melamed 1977; Rebesco 1981). Several methods that have proved effective are: allowing children to view the hospital areas where they will be going for tests and procedures; utilizing films and books to explain the experience; and especially encouraging talking, play activities, and puppets to explain procedures and help the child express fears, concerns, confusion, and anger. Finally, health professionals may continue to provide information and support for parents.

The Terminally Ill Child

The leading cause of death in young children is accidents. The second leading cause of death in early childhood is from complications of severe congenital anomalies of the central nervous system or defects in the heart and circulatory systems, respiratory system, genitourinary system, or musculoskeletal system. The third leading cause is from neoplasms or cancer. Parents usually understand the possibility that a cancer or congenital anomaly will make their child's life expectancy short. Most still hope, however, that surgery, improved medical techniques, protection from infections, or a miracle will give their child additional years of life. In such circumstances, caretakers need accurate information and support. A psychological or psychiatric referral may be needed to help parents cope with their anticipated loss and the attendant problems of guilt and marital stress.

Children of this age have only a vague concept of their own death. The major feeling the child has about death is the anticipation of and fear of losing things and people (Gordon 1981). Often the child will ask questions reflecting this concern with separation—"When I die can I take my dog with me?" It is difficult to assess the kinds of support and intervention that are needed and desired by a terminally ill child. Each child needs to be considered individually. The response to the illness may in part be a function of the disease itself. A leukemic child, for example, may feel at times energetic and at times too weak to engage in physical activity of any type. A child with sarcoma may have trouble relating to others because of the physical abnormality (Gordon 1981). Clearly, denial of the illness to the child or family is destructive. Spinetta, Rigler, and Karon (1974) demonstrated that children who are terminally ill are aware of the upset and increasing isolation of staff and family, even when the illness and impending death have never been discussed. Giving the child permission to talk about the illness decreases the sense of isolation and alienation and reduced the feeling that the illness is too terrible to discuss.

SUMMARY

Early childhood is a period of increased independence and growth in cognitive abilities. The child is capable of conversing with parents. This leads to further expressions of autonomy and more power struggles. In addition, for the first time, people outside the family begin to influence the child. Peer relationships develop around play activities. Socialization involves the balance between learning about personal needs and desires and meeting the rules of social networks. Much of family activity involves the stabilization of care routines—sleeping, eating, and the implementation of safety procedures. Medical procedures and preparation for hospitalization should be based on the child's cognitive abilities and concerns with separation. Contacts with health professionals often involve the treatment of either infections or accidents. During these contacts the health professional may educate caretakers about health-promotion methods and accident prevention.

REFERENCES

Ainsworth, M.D.S. *Infancy in Uganda: Infant Care and the Growth of Love.* Baltimore, Md.: Johns Hopkins University Press, 1967.

Baumruid, D. "Child care practices anteceding three patterns of preschool behavior." *Genetic Psychology Monographs,* 1967, 75:43–88.

Belsky, J., and Sternberg, L. D. "The effects of daycare: A critical review." *Child Development,* 1978, 49:920–949.

Bernstein, A. C., and Cowan, P. A. "Children's concepts of how people get babies." *Child Development,* 1975, 46:77–91.

Bibace, R., and Walsh, M. E. "Developmental stages in children's conceptions of illness." In G. C. Stone, F. Cohen and N. E. Adler (Eds.), *Health Psychology—A Handbook.* San Francisco: Jossey-Bass, 1980.

Billingham, K. A. "The behavioral manifestations of fear of success with women and the modification of such behaviors via a modeling procedure." Doctoral dissertation, DePaul University, Chicago, 1978.

Brocken, C. "Behavior Through the Life Cycle: Early Childhood Development." Unpublished manuscript, Rush Medical College, Chicago, 1981.

Brodie, B. "Views of healthy children toward illness." *American Journal of Public Health,* 1974, 64:1156–1159.

Campbell, J. D. "Illness is a point of view: the development of childrens's concepts of illness." *Child Development,* 1975, 46:92–100.

Chess, S., Thomas, A., and Birch, H. O. "Behavioral problems revisited." In S. Chess and Birch (Eds.), *Annual Progress in Child Psychiatry and Child Development.* New York: Brunner/Mazel, 1968.

Chinn, P. *Child Health Maintenance.* St. Louis: C. V. Mosby Co., 1974.

Erikson, E. H. *Childhood and Society.* 2nd Ed. New York: Norton, 1963.

Feldman, H. S. "Behavior through the Life Cycle: Sexual Development—Infancy Through Aging." Unpublished manuscript, Rush Medical College, Chicago, 1981.

Flavell, J. H. *Cognitive Development.* Englewood Cliffs, N.J.: Prentice-Hall, 1977.

Freiberg, K. L. *Human Development: A Life Span Approach.* Belmont, Calif.: Wadsworth, 1979.

Gellert, E. "Children's conceptions of the content and functions of the human body." *Genetic Psychology Monographs,* 1962, 65:293–405.

Gold, D., and Andres, D. "Relations between maternal employment and development of nursery school children." *Canadian Journal of Behavioral Science,* 1978, 10:116–129.

Gold, D., Andres, D., and Glorieux, J. "The development of Francophone nursery school children with employed and nonemployed mothers." *Canadian Journal of Behavioral Science,* 1979, 1:169–173.

Goldberg, R. J. *Maternal Time Use and Preschool Performance.* Paper presented at the Society for Research in Child Development, New Orleans, La., March, 1977.

Goldsmith, C. H. "The effect of different compliance distributions on the planning and statistical analyses of therapeutic trials." In D. L. Sackett and R. B. Haynes (Eds.), *Compliance with Therapeutic Regimens.* Baltimore, Md.: Johns Hopkins University Press, 1966.

Gordon, L. B. "Behavior Through the Life Cycle: Cognitive Development." Unpublished manuscript, Rush Medical College, Chicago, 1981.

Hartley, R. E., Hardesty, F., and Gorfein, D. S. "Children's perceptions and impression of sex preferences." *Child Development,* 1962, 33:221–227.

Hartup, W. W., and Zook, E. A. "Sex-role preferences in three- and four-year-old children." *Journal of Consulting Psychology,* 1960, 24:420–426.

Hetherington, E. M. "Effects of father absence on personality development in adolescent daughters." *Developmental Psychology,* 1972, 7:313–326.

_____. "Divorce: A child's perspective," *American Psychologist,* 1979, 34 (10):851–858.

Hetherington, E. M., Cox, M., and Cox, R. "The aftermath of divorce." In J. H. Stevens, Jr., and M. Matthews (Eds.), *Mother-Child, Father-Child Relations.* Washington, D.C.: National Association for the Education of Young Children, 1978.

Hetherington, E. M., and Parke, K. *Child Psychology,* New York: McGraw-Hill, 1975.

Hoffman, L. W. "Effects of maternal employment on the child — A review of the research." *Developmental Psychology,* 1974, 10:204–228.

——. "Maternal employment: 1979." *American Psychologist,* 1979, 34(10): 859–865.

Kagan, J. "Family experience and the child's development." *American Psychologist,* 1979, 34(10):886–891.

Kagan, J., Kearsley, R. B., and Zelazo, P. R. *Infancy: Its Place in Human Development.* Cambridge, Mass.: Harvard University Press, 1978.

Kagan, J., Lapidus, D., and Moore, M. "Infant antecedents of later cognitive functioning." *Child Development,* 1978, 49:1005–1023.

Kagan, J., and Moss, H. A. *Birth to Maturity.* New York: John Wiley and Sons, 1972.

Kolodny, R. C., Masters, W. H., and Johnson, V. E. *Textbook of Sexual Medicine.* Boston: Little, Brown & Co., 1979.

Kreitler, H., and Kreitler, S. "Children's concepts of sex and birth." *Child Development,* 1966, 37:363–378.

Lamb, M. E. "Parental influences and the father's role." *American Psychologist,* 1979, 34(10):938–943.

Lansky, L. M. "Some comments on Ward's (1968) 'Variance of sex-role preferences among boys and girls.'" *Psychological Reports,* 1968, 23:649–650.

Lynn, D. B. *The Father: His Role in Child Development.* Belmont, Calif.: Wadsworth, 1974.

Marsden, D. *Mothers Alone: Poverty and the Fatherless Family.* London: Allan Lane, Penguin Press, 1969.

Mechanic, D. "The influence of mothers on their children's health attitudes and behaviors." *Pediatrics,* 1964, 33:444–453.

Melamed, B. G. "Psychological preparation for hospitalization." In S. Rachman (Ed.), *Contributions to Medical Psychology.* New York: Pergamon Press, 1977.

Moss, H. A., and Robson, K. S. "Maternal influences on early social-visual behavior." *Child Development,* 1968, 39:401–408.

Murray, R. B., and Zentner, J. P. *Nursing Assessment and Health Promotion Through the Life Span,* 2nd Ed. Englewood Cliffs, N.J.: Prentice-Hall, 1979.

Mussen, P. H. *The Psychological Development of the Child,* 2nd Ed. Englewood Cliffs, N.J.: Prentice-Hall, 1973.

Mussen, P. H., Conger, J. J., Kagan, J., and Gewitz, J. *Psychological Development: A Life Span Approach.* New York: Harper & Row, 1979.

Nagy, M. "Children's birth theories." *Journal of Genetic Psychology,* 1953a, 83:217–226.

_____. "Children's conceptions of some bodily functions." *Journal of Genetic Psychology,* 1953b, 83:199–216.

_____. "The meaning of death." In H. Feifel (Ed.), *The Meaning of Death.* New York: McGraw-Hill, 1959.

Palmer, B. B., and Lewis, C. E. *Development of Health Attitudes and Behaviors.* Paper presented at annual meeting of the American School Health Association, Denver, Colorado, October, 1975.

Patterson, G. R. *Families.* Champaign, Ill.: Research Press, 1975.

_____. *Living with Children.* Champaign, Ill.: Research Press, 1976.

Rebesco, M. P. "Behavior Through the Life Cycle: Psychological Challenges of Pediatric Hospitalization." Unpublished manuscript, Rush Medical College, Chicago, 1981.

Reese, A. N., and Palmer, H. I. "Factors related to change in mental test performance." *Developmental Psychology Monograph,* 1970, 3 (2, part 2).

Schwarz, J. C. "Childhood origins of psychopathology." *American Psychologist,* 1979, 34(10):879–885.

Sherman, J. A. *On the Psychology of Women.* Springfield, Ill.: C. C. Thomas, 1975.

Skinner, B. F. *Verbal Behavior.* New York: Appleton-Century-Crofts, 1957.

Spinetta, J. J., Rigler, D., and Karon, M. "Personal space as a measure of a dying child's sense of isolation." *Journal of Consulting and Clinical Psychology,* 1974, 42:751–757.

Steward, M., and Regalbuto, B. A. "Do doctors know what children know?" *American Journal of Orthopsychiatry,* 1975, 45:146–149.

Tessman, L. H. *Children of Parting Parents.* New York: Aronson, 1978.

Wallerstein, J. S., and Kelly, J. B. "The effects of parental divorce: Experiences of the preschool child." *Journal of the American Academy of Child Psychiatry,* 1975, 14:600–616.

Westman, J. (Ed.) *Individual Differences in Children.* New York: John Wiley and Sons, 1973.

Wolman, B. B., and Money, J. (Eds.) *Handbook of Human Sexuality.* Englewood Cliffs, N.J.: Prentice-Hall, 1980.

Yarrow, L. J., Rubenstein, J. L. and Pederson, F. A. *Infant and Environment: Early Cognitive and Motivational Development.* Washington, D.C.: Hemisphere, 1975.

LATE CHILDHOOD DEVELOPMENT

INTRODUCTION

Late childhood spans the years from 6 to 12, the period when the child is in primary school. It is also a time when the child's world opens up through experiences at school, exploration of the neighborhood and community, and books and fantasies of adventure. The most vivid memories of childhood are usually from this time period: explorations with best friends, school activities, favorite teachers, family traditions, chores, sports, long summers, and secret hiding places. Many of the literary works on childhood encompass the feelings, adventures, and conflicts of this period – *Oliver Twist* by Dickens, *Tom Sawyer* by Mark Twain. This is a time of considerable development physically, cognitively, emotionally, and socially.

Late childhood is sometimes divided into two age groups: juveniles, from ages 6 to 9; and preadolescents, from approximately 9 to the beginning of puberty at about age 10 or 11. Preadolescence is also called prepubescence and is characterized in both sexes by an increase in hormone production preparatory to eventual physical maturity. During this time period, physical growth is slower than it was in early childhood and slower than it will be adolescence. The child of this age, like the younger child, will usually see the health professional because of infection or accident. In addition, the school becomes an important assessment agent and may make referrals for problems not previously identified by caretakers, such as mild hearing problems or the need for reading glasses or problems directly related to academic performance (dyslexia or hyperactivity, for example). Illness also causes greater disruption for the school-age child than for the young child. When school-age children are ill during the months from September to June, they suffer academic loss and deprivation of peer-group and social interactions. Children may hide symptoms of illness in order to go to school to be with friends or not miss an important activity. Others may feign symptoms to avoid attending school. Fortunately, because of the greater physiological development of older children, illness is generally less prevalent in late childhood than in early childhood.

Developmental Tasks

The range of development tasks that are the focus for this age group demonstrates the increasing variety of roles the child fulfills in the family, at school, and in the community:

1. Decreasing dependence upon family and more satisfying relationships with other adults and peers.
2. Becoming a more active and cooperative family participant.
3. Learning how to handle strong feelings and impulses appropriately.
4. Learning basic concepts and knowing how to reason and solve problems.
5. Adjusting to changing body image and self-concept and coming to terms with sex-role identification.
6. Arranging socially acceptable ways of getting money and saving it for later satisfaction.
7. Developing a positive attitude toward one's own and other social, racial, economic, and religious groups.

THE FAMILY

The child in this age group is simultaneously developing a more active and cooperative role within the family and establishing important relationships outside of the family. If the mother has not yet become employed outside the home, she very likely will do so when the children begin to attend school (Hoffman 1979). The effects of maternal employment as well as the father's role in the family have been found to differ for boys and girls during late childhood. The health professional should be aware of the effects of divorce and subsequent loss of daily contact with a parent. Sibling relationships also become particularly important, and although siblings influence children under the age of 6, their relationship with the school-age child is more intense and complex.

Maternal Employment

When children enter school, the problem of child care is, obviously, considerably diminished. Children spend a smaller portion of their waking time with their mothers, and even in homes with one parent as a full-time homemaker, the father becomes more involved in socialization tasks. Father's role is often intensified in the family in which the mother works outside the home. Research indicates that in such families, although the woman maintains the larger share, the husband participates more in housework and child care (Hoffman 1979). The father is less likely to have a second job and will thus have more time for his family. Older children are more likely to have household responsibilities and more freedom in handling their own money, both of which have been found to contribute to self-esteem (Smokler 1975). The data suggest that the employed mother, except when guilt intervenes, is more likely to encourage independence in her children. Studies of lower socioeconomic populations and one-parent families have found that employed mothers are more likely to have structured rules for their children and to be consistent in putting theory into practice (Hoffman 1974).

Sons and daughters have been found to respond differently to maternal employment. The family of a mother employed outside the home may offer much to increase a daughter's academic and occupational competence and to contribute to positive adjustment. Daughters from such homes are more likely to admire their mothers, to hold the female role in high esteem, and to have higher occupational achievement than daughters of mothers who work in the home (Hoffman 1979). In addition, husbands of employed women are more likely to approve of and encourage competence in females (Hoffman 1974). Research has shown that high-achieving women often have a background that includes a close relationship with a warm and encouraging father, and the greater participation of the father in child care would seem likely to provide this (Billingham 1978). The research on sons of employed women presents a more complex picture. Like daughters, school-age sons of mothers who work outside the home are less stereotyped in their views of both sexes and tend to see women as more competent than do sons of mothers who stay home. In addition, these sons have better social and personality adjustment scores on various standard measures and sometimes higher academic scores (Gold and Andres 1978; Hoffman 1974). Other studies, however, show that these positive results are related to the social class of the family. In a lower class family, maternal employment results in lower achievement performance and a strain in the father-son relationship (Hoffman 1979). In such cases, the son often interprets the mother's employment as a reflection of the father's inadequacy. The data for the middle class show no strain in the father-son relationship, but these sons may also score lower on intellectual indices. Clearly there is need for further research in this area to determine what factors in full-time mothering affect the academic performance of sons and how long term the effects are.

Father's Role

As the child ages, the father's role increases. Unfortunately, inferences about paternal influences on older children depend largely on studies of father's absence. The applicability of these studies is limited because it is impossible to differentiate between factors that relate to paternal influence (lack of parent figure and male model) and factors that do not (mother's economic and emotional distress) (Lamb 1979). However, it is noteworthy that Blanchard and Biller (1971) found that the effects of psychological father absence (which occurs when for professional or attitudinal reasons, fathers seldom spend time with their children) and those of physical father absence (through divorce) were qualitatively similar. As in most studies of father absence, Blanchard and Biller focused on the effects of paternal deprivation on sex-role development in boys, and like most other investigations, their research showed deviant or deficient sex-role development. Among girls, father absence appears to predict dissatisfaction with and maladjustment in the female role, as well as difficulties in interactions with males (Hetherington 1965, 1972). However, these effects in girls are often not evident until adolescence. In boys, the negative effects of father absence are apparent much earlier (Lamb 1979).

Relationships with Siblings

As the child develops socially and cognitively, relationships with peers become more sophisticated. Likewise, the capabilities that contribute to peer relationships at this age also make sibling relationships more complex. Much research has been done on the effects of sex-status among siblings, the effects of position in the family, and the relationship between academic performance and firstborns. I will discuss sex-status among siblings in the section on sexual development later in this chapter. The effects of power relationships among siblings are well known. Firstborns display more high-power tactics; children born second tend to be more counterreactive, even aggressive. More girls with older sisters reported a desire to change positions than did any other group, mostly because of issues of power tactics (Sutton-Smith and Rosenberg 1970). Second-born children or only children have been found to be more overtly aggresive and tend to participate in more dangerous sports (Nisbett 1968). Firstborns and only children are generally more achievement-oriented and tend to get better grades (Altus 1962). Firstborns are overrepresented in colleges, especially those with more selective admissions criteria (Bayer 1966), as well as in positions of eminence (Schachter 1963). From this research, it is clear that postion in the family has multiple effects. In addition, when considering modeling effects on personality development, it is important to account for the influence of older siblings as well as parental models. Finally, when educating caretakers about accident prevention, it may be important to note that second-born children tend to take greater risks, and younger siblings often attempt behaviors beyond their capabilities because of the influence of older siblings.

PHYSICAL DEVELOPMENT

Physical growth in late childhood is slower than it was in early childhood and will be in adolescence. Between the ages of 6 and 12, the child's proportions become more adultlike. Arms and legs get longer, the abdomen flattens, and the shoulders and trunk broaden. The size of the head changes very little, measuring 53.34 cm (21 inches) in circumference, but facial proportions are altered—features become more distinct and less babylike. The child of this age group tends to gain an average of 3.15 kg (7 pounds) yearly. The average weight for a 6-year-old male is 21.60 kg (48 pounds) and the average height is 116.84 cm (46 inches). Height gains are about 5.08 cm (2 inches) yearly. By age 12, the average child should weigh approximately 36–40.5 kg (80 to 90 pounds) and stand about 147.32 cm (58 inches) in height. Females tend to be smaller and shorter than males until the ages of 11 or 12 when they often weigh more and are taller. Black children tend to be smaller in weight and height than white children (Murray and Zentner 1979). It is important to recognize that weight and height vary considerably among children this age and are highly dependent on genetic and environmental factors.

During late childhood, temperature, pulse, and respiration gradually approach adult norms. Average temperatures are 98°F to 98.6°F (36.7°C to 37°C); resting pulse is 60 to 76; and respiration rate is 18 to 21 per minute. Systolic blood pressure averages 94 to 112; diastolic blood pressure is 56 to 60 millimeters of mercury. Late childhood usually begins with the shedding of deciduous teeth in preparation for the permanent ones. Throughout this 6-year period, deciduous teeth are lost and permanent teeth are gained, until by age 12 most children have twenty-eight of the eventual thirty-two permanent teeth, lacking only the wisdom teeth that may or may not appear during adolesence. By age 6 or 7, visual acuity approaches 20/20 and peripheral vision is fully developed. Roughly 25 percent of school-age children need to wear glasses (Holm and Wiltz 1973). Neuromuscular changes occur with skeletal development, resulting in sufficient neuromuscular coordination for the child to learn most desired skills. Basic neuromuscular mechanisms are developed at age 6 and muscular coordination improves steadily thereafter.

Annual physical check-ups allow a steady evaluation of growth and physical development. The health professional needs to obtain accurate growth charts that have norms based on sex and race.

COGNITIVE DEVELOPMENT

An understanding of cognitive development in the older child involves not only an understanding of cognitive abilities, but also awareness of how these abilities are measured by intelligence tests. It is important for the health professional to recognize that cognitive abilities determine the way in which children understand illness and view death.

Piaget

Piaget calls the stage that encompasses ages 7 through 11 the concrete-operational stage. During this time the deficiencies of the preoperational period are, to a great extent, overcome. The concrete-operational child's thinking is characterized by decentration and an understanding of the concept of conservation. The concept of conservation may be illustrated by the following example: Assume that equal amounts of water are placed in two glasses – one is tall and thin and one short and stout. The young child, in the preoperational stage, would say that the tall glass has more water in it. The concrete-operational child, however, could understand that both glasses have equal amounts of water. This is because the older child has the ability to transform the dimension of height into the different dimension of volume and back again. Understanding the concept of conservation, the child perceives that the volume of water is conserved and maintained regardless of the shape of the glass (Piaget and Inhelder 1969). Decentration means that the child can leave his or her own perspective and view the situation from another vantage point. The concrete-operational child goes beyond immediate appearance to infer from available evidence that the quantities are the same. The child can recognize that the task requires conceptual, rather than perceptual, judgment. In contrast, the younger preoperational child makes judgments on the basis of appearance. In addition, the concrete-operational child has the cognitive capability of reversibility. This refers to the quality of the thinking process that allows steps to be retraced, actions canceled, and the original situation restored. Using the concept of reversibility, the sequence of steps in problem solving may be interrupted and returned to the beginning in order to start over (Piaget and Inhelder 1969).

The concrete-operational child succeeds in other tasks in which preoperational children fail. Older children have a more advanced notion of classes in an abstract sense, and they can sort objects on the basis of shape, color, and size. These children are also better at understanding relationships between classes and subclasses, recognizing that an object can belong to both simultaneously. Serialization of objects is no longer difficult. Primarily, this age group is capable of elementary logical process – or what Piaget refers to as operations – reasoning deductively, from premise to conclusion, in a logical way. However, this process is still limited and elementary and deals only with concrete events and perceptions. The child is not able to think in abstract terms or reason about verbal or hypothetical propositions until adolescence.

These new cognitive abilities influence the ways in which the child relates to others. Observation, comparison, and comprehension of others assume an important part in children's lives. They are eager to avoid self-contradiction, a common phenomenon in previous phases, and they attempt to understand variations in behavioral expectations. Preadolescents from the age of 9 to 11 generally become more interested in the rules that regulate their lives. They examine rules for all their details. They inquire into the meaning of the parts in order to establish verifiable relationships and guarantee themselves a sense of permanency. In addition, the child's awareness of social reciprocity and equality carries over into concepts of fairness and justice. Justice requires fair punishment. The child expects equality in punishment and exact compensation for damage done, and considers doing to another exactly what was done to him/herself to be fair judgment. These concepts of orderliness and fairness generalize into the beginnings of social consciousness and influence conceptualizations of illness and death.

Intelligence Tests

As measures of cognitive abilities, intelligence tests have been constructed to examine the ability to think in abstract terms and to reason, together with the ability to use these functions for adaptive purposes. Piaget regarded intelligence as a specific instance of adaptive behavior, of coping with the environment and organizing thought and action (Piaget 1926). All tests of intelligence contain items that tap the kinds of functions with which Piaget was concerned—problem solving, reasoning, abstract thinking. The scores from these tests have been very widely used in clinical evaluations, in educational counseling, and in school placement because the scores tell immediately where an individual ranks intellectually compared to others of the same age. However, the use of intelligence tests that emphasize individual differences and rely on language skills has recently raised a number of important social questions and become a source of major conflict. One critical problem involves the use of these tests for children from severely deprived backgrounds. The tests have also sometimes been inappropriately given to bilingual children. Some of the issues raised involve questions of the hereditary determinants of intelligence, racial and socioeconomic differences in intellectual test performance, and the stability of intellectual performance over time—from early childhood to adolescence, for example. Consequently, the uses of test scores are being reexamined and modified.

Conceptualizations of Illness

The increased cognitive sophistication of the older child becomes obvious when his or her understanding of illness is compared to the younger child's. Evidence of concrete-operational thinking is present in the older child's attempts to make logical sense out of all the data of concrete reality. In defining illness, the child no longer focuses on a single factor, but mentions multiple symptoms (Bibace and Walsh 1980). Furthermore, the child uses concrete data that are more directly related to the illness. Children mention externally visible bodily processes, such as breathing. The child is also less egocentric and describes illness as a more general phenomenon. This decrease in egocentricity also allows children to differentiate between themselves and the world so that they are able to make a connection between the source of the illness and the illness itself. Older children are also able to internalize; they describe the illness as being, in general, inside the body. However, children of this age are not concerned with what is happening inside their bodies in the way adolescents would be concerned. Rather, their concern is in how the illness became internalized—for example, "Did I swallow some germs?" Because the child is still unable to differentiate mind and body, bad or immoral behavior is seen as just as likely as contact with dirt or germs to cause illness. The child's understanding of the concept of reversibility results in understanding that a person who is sick can become well and vice versa (Bibace and Walsh 1980).

These findings should be used in the context of other variables such as individual differences and psychosocial factors. An initial assessment (through an interview) should be made of the child's cognitive abilities in relation to an emotionally neutral problem. Then the more stress-inducing information regarding medical procedures, diagnosis, and treatment may be presented—in a way that fits the cognitive capabilities of the child.

Conceptualizations of Death

In Nagy's (1959) work on children's conceptualizations of death, she found that children ages 5 to 9 personify death. Unlike younger children, children of this age acknowledge death's existence but make an active effort to keep it distant. These children feel that "only those die whom the death-man carries off" (Gordon 1981). They express an increasing sense that death exists in reality and that it is undesirable. After age 9, children understand that death is the cessation of life and that it is a universal process that is inevitable for all. This understanding implies the concepts of reversibility (focusing on the transformations of states) and decentration (leaving one's own perspective and seeing things from another vantage point or perspective). According to Piaget and Inhelder (1969), children from 5 to 9 often view death as punishment for disobedience or retaliation for some sexual or aggressive wishes and not as a result of natural causes. They feel that the bad die before the good; the good return to life, the bad stay dead. A recent longitudinal study by White, Elsom, and Prawatt (1978) confirmed Piaget's hypothesis.

In conclusion, the increased cognitive skills of the older child are apparent in several ways. The child demonstrates a certain level of problem solving, examines social rules, and shows an increased ability to relate. The health professional is likely to obtain more accurate descriptions of symptoms and pains from members of this age group. Procedures and treatments may also be more easily explained and understood by the child. Finally, the older child has greater capacities for becoming involved in accident prevention and health promotion.

SEXUAL DEVELOPMENT

The sexual development of the older child continues to follow a sequence based on earlier childhood experiences. There is a greater awareness of body image, sensual/erotic needs, and sex-role identification.

The 6-year-old has a greater awareness of sex differences in body structure than does the younger child. Children of this age continue to investigate and question adults about sex. It is not uncommon for them to ask about intercourse, to accept the notion of a baby growing inside the mother, and to understand the concept of life beginning with a seed (Feldman 1981). Often the 6-year-old will have an intense desire to have a new baby in the family to hold and play with.

When the child reaches 7 years of age exploration and sex play diminishes once again. Children become more concerned with sex roles than anatomy. They tend to be self-conscious about their bodies and avoid bodily exposure and being touched by others (Wolman and Money 1980). It is not uncommon, however, for strong boy/girl friendships to develop that incorporate the concept of marriage as an eventual outcome (Kolodny, Masters, and Johnson 1979). Throughout the rest of late childhood, children experience both autoerotic and interpersonal erotic sensations that provide a groundwork for later erotic experiences. These include self-exploration, games with peers, and nurturant contacts with adults. Masturbation is common, but not always erotic in nature. It is often a source of security, especially in boys (Feldman 1981). Romances develop and are accepted by girls, but cause ostracizing among boys. Children begin to learn about sex from older children and often experiment in ways that are typically not aggressive and contribute to their knowledge (Wolman and Money 1980).

Although many cultures allow children to observe adults in sexual activity, ours does not. Nevertheless, children's ideas about marriage and relationships are often obtained through observing parents. Parents often unknowingly convey their attitudes about sex through tone of voice and avoidance of topics.

Sex-Role Identification

The family has strong influences on the sex-role identification of its members. For example, Rosenberg and Sutton-Smith (1964) found that in two-children families, boys with older sisters tend to exhibit more female behaviors than do boys with older brothers. On the other hand, girls with older brothers tend to exhibit more masculine behaviors than do girls with older sisters. More recent research (Bem 1974; Bem, Martyna, and Watson 1976) suggests that the ability to be flexible in cross-sexed behaviors is more adaptive than stringent sex-role identification. The effects of father-absence on the sex-role identification of boys has already been reviewed. However, other factors, such as the age of the child when the father leaves (Hetherington 1965) and the presence of older brothers, uncles and other male models, often diminish any negative effects (Sherman 1975). In addition, although there are disadvantages to raising children in single-parent families, such children make more satisfactory adjustments than those reared in unhappy, strife-ridden intact families (Sherman 1975).

PERSONALITY DEVELOPMENT

As the child ages, issues concerning personality become more complex. In this section, a review of the viewpoints of Freud and

Erikson will be followed by a presentation of the process of identification through modeling and a discussion of specific personality traits (such as aggression). Socialization through peer-group association will be the final topic.

Freud

According to Freud, at about the age of 5, following the resolution of the Oepidal complex, children of both sexes pass into a period called latency. Latency is not considered a stage of psychosexual development because the libido is channeled into activities such as school, interpersonal relationships with children of the same age, sports, and so on. Freud wrote little about this period in life, although other psychoanalytic writers have placed considerable emphasis on it (Sainoff 1976).

Erikson

Erikson termed the period of development from ages 6 to 10 as the period of industry versus inferiority. A child of this age, according to Erikson, must accomplish five major tasks: (1) development of intellectual and academic skills and the motivation to master them, (2) crystallization of sex-role identification, (3) increased autonomy and independence, (4) development of moral standards, and (5) creation of coping strategies to deal appropriately with anxiety and conflict. Children are very physically and intellectually active during this time. They are also starting to learn the rules of society and how to function in it. Girls tend to do better than boys in every area. A number of studies indicate that the general level of behavior, academic performance, and coordination of girls exceeds that of their male counterparts (Mussen et al. 1979).

The Effects of Modeling

Observers have long understood that children acquire attitudes, values, and patterns of social behavior by direct tuition. An extensive body of developmental research examines modeling—the indirect imitation of others such as parents, teachers, and peers. In a series of experiments done with children, Bandura and colleagues demonstrated that subjects allowed to observe an unusual set of responses performed by another individual (model) in a situation, tend to exhibit these same behaviors when placed in the situation themselves. Several factors have been found to promote modeling behavior: There must be some type of identification with the model; the more socially powerful model has more chance of being imitated; behavior for which the model is rewarded is most likely to be imitated; and verbal explanations of behaviors also increase the likelihood of imitation.

Bandura's early work (Bandura, Ross, and Ross 1961) demonstrated the extent to which aggression may be transmitted to children through exposure to aggressive adult models. Later studies have shown that nurturing behavior modification of fears, social responsibility, and diverse skills such as coping with test anxiety and promoting achievement tasks may all be transmitted to children through modeling (Bandura 1965, 1969, 1971; Billingham 1978; Sarason 1972). Modeling is not only an important concept for understanding personality development, but it can also be a useful tool in helping children cope with illness and manage behaviors on the pediatric unit (Melamed 1977).

Personality Traits

The four personality traits that have received the most attention in developmental research are aggression, dependency, anxiety, and achievement motivation. The tendency to indulge in aggressive behavior has been found to be fairly stable throughout childhood and more prevalent in boys than girls (Mussen et al. 1979). The tendency of boys to engage in more physical aggression than girls is probably related to the fact that boys are rewarded for aggressive activities more often than girls (Sherman 1975). Mussen (1973) believed that the amount and intensity of aggression in children is related to past reinforcement of aggressive behavior, availability and influence of aggressive models, and the degree to which aggressive behaviors in the past have relieved feelings of anger, hurt, and sadness. Research has consistently demonstrated that adult tolerance of aggression increases its incidence and punishment reduces its incidence (Bandura 1965). Bandura and colleagues noted that the influence of punishment in reducing aggression may be short-term, particularly if the punishment is also aggressive, thus giving the child an additional model for aggression.

In contrast to aggression, which is more stable in boys, dependency tends to be more stable in girls. Most research on the stability of dependency suggests that dependency decreases with age (Mussen et al. 1979). Other researchers suggest that dependency remains constant but changes in the way it is manifested. That is, as the child grows older, dependency shifts in focus from caretakers to peers. There are marked individual differences among children with regard to anxiety, the third trait. Pathological anxiety may reflect harsh socialization procedures, but the normal fears of children may only represent modeling of another person's fear responses. Support for this possibility includes the demonstration that fear may be reduced when children are exposed to unfearful models (Bandura 1971) and that children tend to have the same fears as their parents (Mussen et al. 1979). The last trait, achievement motivation, also develops in response to reward and modeling (Hoffman 1979). In addition, achievement motivation appears to be related to the child's degree of independence and sex differences in achievement appear after the age of 12 (Billingham 1978).

Socialization

Social relationships during the school years are more extensive, intense, and influential than those of earlier years. From roughly ages 7 to 12, children are strongly concerned with their peer gang, an informal group with a fairly rapid turnover in membership. Later on, between the ages of 10 and 14, more highly structured groups with formal organization and membership requirements become more salient, especially among middle-class children. Both boys and girls organize their groups around learning new skills, mastery, trying new roles, and secrecy. Peer groups also promote self-concept formation among individual members (Billingham 1981). Social status among peers is a function of age, sex, and appearance, and peer conformity increases markedly during these years. The fact that peer rules are all-important reflects the child's need for structure and control. In fact, the group may have no apparent purpose besides the organization itself.

The personality characteristics associated with popularity during these years parallel those associated with preschool popularity— friendliness, sociability, outgoingness, sensitivity to the needs and feelings of other children, and enthusiasm. The expression of inappropriate aggression is negatively correlated with popularity, although according to some studies, responding aggressively when provoked is associated with peer acceptance.

In conclusion, personality development for late childhood involves the evolution of greater individual differences, more independence from the family, and increased influence of peers.

HEALTH CARE CONSIDERATIONS

The major concerns in the medical care of school-age children relate to adjustment to bodily changes, injuries (as a result of engaging in physical activity that exceeds capabilities), behavior problems and difficulties in social adjustment, and delayed development due to either psychological difficulties or organic pathology. Medical treatment in late childhood tends to generate fears of bodily harm. This fear is primarily the result of fear of punishment for impulses or feelings, the child's increased ability to conceptualize and anticipate, and the tendency to engage in fantasies of danger. The health professional should not be misled by the child's stoic front and should encourage the child to air these fears and concerns. Showing an understanding of the child's anxiety and willingness to help cope with it may facilitate expression in the case of the child who is unable to talk about fear (Gordon 1981). Sometimes fear may be allayed by fully explaining all medical procedures. A child may also have a specific intense fear of anesthesia, as it represents loss of voluntary control and even death. Murray and Zentner (1979) suggested that, in view of the high value children place on the body and their anxiety about mutilation, any elective surgery that must be done should be performed before the age of 4 if at all possible or delayed until after age 7. As the health professional shows interest in the child's healthy functions, the child will gradually be able to admit to a few symptoms. The professional may then present problems without creating excessive anxiety and in the process establish a very nice rapport with the child.

Special Health Needs

The school-age child is similar to the younger child in nutritional needs and in the need for health promotion through accident prevention. For the older child, referrals begin to come from school. Also self-destructive behavior starts to appear. Finally, sexual issues involving the school-age child need to be dealt with differently.

Although caloric requirements per unit of body weight decrease as the child ages, nutritional requirements remain relatively greater than for adults. The juvenile needs approximately 16 calories per kg (35 calories per pound) daily. By age 12 these requirements decrease to 14 calories per kg (30 calories per pound). The total caloric requirement range is from about 1,600 to 2,200 calories daily. Protein requirements for growth are approximately one-half gram per kg or 50 to 80 grams of protein daily. Vitamin and mineral requirements are similar to those for the preschool child.

As for the younger child, accident prevention continues to be important. The increased cognitive abilities of school-age children make the task somewhat easier in that they can begin to follow safety rules and may even instruct younger children on proper behavior. Unfortunately, school contact may have two negative effects regarding health care. First, the child comes in contact with many other children and becomes more susceptible to sore throats and colds with lung and ear complications. Second, both peer contact and parental modeling at around age 10 make this a critical period for discussions regarding smoking and drug and alcohol abuse (Matarazzo 1980).

Sexual Concerns

The health professional may play an important role in correcting misconceptions and myths about the sexual behavior of older children. Often parents respond to the behavior of their children in one of two polarized ways. They either exaggerate the child's sexual behavior and see it as abnormal or they tend to deny what is obvious. Communication with younger children, particularly victims of molestation or sexual abuse, may be slowly established through unstructured play situations. In such cases, dolls may express feelings, concerns, and interests that the child cannot express directly. For the older child direct verbalization may be effective, but the health professional must be careful of the dual meanings attached to some words. For example, if asked "How did you feel?" the child may understand "feel" in the sense of "touch" and will not respond with an expression of emotions. In these discussions, a sense of support and understanding may be achieved through tone of voice and an accepting manner.

Dealing with Death

Numerous studies have been done on chidren's responses to the deaths of others. The death of a parent or other significant adult in the child's life is hardest to cope with because of the sudden loss of gratification of physical and emotional needs. With the loss of a sibling, the child may, for a long time, dread even minor illness (Gordon 1981). Violent deaths are the most difficult to cope with. Grandparent's deaths are easiest because they are not seen as unnatural or terrifying. A loss in childhood that is unmourned leaves undealt-with emotions that stay active and influence the way in which the child copes with feelings and establishes relationships with other people (Gordon 1981).

Spinetta (1975) examined the psychological issues of death for terminally ill children in this age group and found that children understand the seriousness of their illnesses. Fatally ill children ages 6 to 10 do not necessarily talk about death but do show severe anxiety about bodily threat and bodily function. These children tend to express great concerns about hospital personnel and procedures and anxiety about hospitalization. The health professional needs to talk with the terminally ill child, moving at the child's speed and talking in a way the child can understand. The professional should offer a full explanation of all procedures, answer all questions, and reassure the child directly and indirectly of emotional support.

SUMMARY

The period of late childhood is characterized by increased reasoning abilities, greater importance of socialization, a more autonomous, active role in the family, and a slowing of physical growth. Distinct individual personalities become more apparent and influence school performance and acceptance with peers. Sex-role identification is also an important goal during this period.

With children this age, the health professional is able to better establish one-to-one relationships, understand symptom reports, and explain medical procedures. Health promotion during late childhood may involve accident prevention, influencing decisions regarding smoking, drinking, or using drugs, and counseling the child regarding sexual issues and death.

REFERENCES

Altus, W. D. "Sibling order and scholastic aptitude." *American Psychologist,* 1962, 17:304.

Bandura, A. "Behavior modification through modeling procedures." In L. Krasner and L. P. Ullman (Eds.), *Research in Behavior Modification.* New York: Holt, Rinehart & Winston, 1965.

_____. *Principles of Behavior Modification.* New York: Holt, Rinehart & Winston, 1969.

_____. "Psychotherapy based on modeling principles." In A. Bergin and S. Garfield (Eds.), *Handbook of Psychotherapy and Behavioral Change.* New York: John Wiley and Sons, 1971.

Bandura, A., Ross, D., and Ross, S. A. "Transmission of aggression through imitation of aggressive models." *Journal of Abnormal and Social Psychology,* 1961, 63:575–582.

Bayer, A. E. "Birth order and college attendance." *Journal of Marriage and Family Living,* 1966, 28:480–484.

Bem, S. L. "The measure of psychological androgyny." *Journal of Consulting and Clinical Psychology,* 1974, 42:155–162.

Bem, S. L., Martyna, W., and Watson, C. "Sex typing and androgyny: Further explorations of the expressive domain." *Journal of Personality and Social Psychology,* 1976, 34:1016–1023.

Bibace, R., and Walsh, M. E. "Developmental stages in children's conceptions of illness." In G. C. Stone, F. Cohen and N. E. Adler (Eds.), *Health Psychology—A Handbook.* San Francisco: Jossey-Bass, 1980.

Billingham, K. A. "The Behavioral Manifestations of Fear of Success with Women and the Modification of such via a Modeling Procedure." Doctoral dissertation, DePaul University, Chicago, 1978.

_____. "Behavior Through the Life Cycle: Adolescent Development." Unpublished manuscript, Rush Medical College, Chicago, 1981.

Blanchard, R. W., and Biller, H. B. "Father availability and academic performance among third-grade boys." *Developmental Psychology,* 1971, 4:301–305.

Feldman, H. S. "Behavior Through the Life Span: Sexual Development—Infancy Through Aging." Unpublished manuscript, Rush Medical College, Chicago, 1981.

Gold, D., and Andres, D. "Relations between maternal employment and development of nursery school children." *Canadian Journal of Behavioral Science,* 1978, 10:116–129.

Gordon, L. B. "Behavior Through the Life Cycle: Cognitive Development." Unpublished manuscript, Rush Medical College, Chicago, 1981.

Hetherington, E. M. "A developmental study of the effects of sex of the dominant parent on sex role preference, identification, and imitation in children." *Journal of Personality and Social Psychology,* 1965, 2:188–194.

_____. "Effects of father absence on personality development in adolescent daughters." *Developmental Psychology,* 1972, 7:313–326.

Hoffman, L. W. "Effects of maternal employment on the child – A review of the research." *Developmental Psychology,* 1974, 10:204–228.

_____. "Maternal employment: 1979." *American Psychologist,* 1979, 34(10): 859–865.

Holm, V., and Wiltz, N. "Childhood." In D. Smith and E. Bierman (Eds.), *The Biologic Ages of Man.* Philadelphia: W. B. Saunders, 1973.

Kolodny, R. C., Masters, W. H., and Johnson, V. E. *Textbook of Sexual Medicine.* Boston: Little, Brown & Co. 1979.

Lamb, M. E. "Paternal influences and the father's role." *American Psychologist,* 1979, 34(10):938–943.

Matarazzo, J. D. "Behavioral health and behavioral medicine: Frontiers for a new health psychology." *American Psychologist,* 1980, 35(9):807–817.

Melamed, B. G. "Psychological preparation for hospitalization." In S. Rachman (Ed.), *Contributions to Medical Psychology.* New York: Pergamon Press, 1977.

Murray, R. B., and Zentner, J. P. *Nursing Assessment and Health Promotion Through the Life Span,* 2nd Ed. Englewood Cliffs, N.J.: Prentice-Hall, 1979.

Mussen, P. H. *The Psychological Development of the Child.* 2nd Ed. Englewood Cliffs, N.J.: Prentice-Hall, 1973.

Mussen, P. H., Conger, J. J., Kagan, J., and Gewitz, J. *Psychological Development: A Life Span Approach.* New York: Harper & Row, 1979.

Nagy, M. "The meaning of death." In H. Feifel (Ed.), *The Meaning of Death.* New York: McGraw-Hill, 1959.

Nisbett, R. W. "Birth order and participation in dangerous sports." *Journal of Personality and Social Psychology,* 1968, 8(4):351–353.

Piaget, J. *The Language and Thought of the Child.* New York: Harcourt, Brace, 1926.

Piaget, J., and Inhelder, B. *The Psychology of the Child.* New York: Basic Books, 1969.

Rosenberg, B. G., and Sutton-Smith, B. "Ordinal position and sex-role identification." *Genetic Psychological Monographs,* 1964, 70:297–328.

Sainoff, C. *Latency.* New York: Jason Aronson, 1976.

Sarason, I. "Experimental approaches to test anxiety." In C. D. Spielberger (Ed.), *Anxiety and Behavior.* Vol. 2. New York: Academic Press, 1972.

Schachter, S. "Birth order, eminence and higher education." *American Sociological Review,* 1963, 28:757–767.

Sherman, J. A. *On the Psychology of Women.* Springfield, Ill.: C. C. Thomas, 1975.

Smokler, C. S. "Self-Esteem in Pre-Adolescent and Adolescent Females." Doctoral dissertation, University of Michigan, 1975. Cited in L. W. Hoffman, 1979.

Spinetta, J. J. "The dying child's awareness of death: A review." In S. Chess and A. Thomas (Eds.), *Annual Progress in Child Psychiatry and Child Development.* New York: Basic Books, 1975.

Sutton-Smith, B., and Rosenberg, B. G. *The Sibling.* Chicago: Holt, Rinehart & Winston, 1970.

White, E. W., Elsom, B., and Prawatt, R. "Children's conceptions of death." *Child Development,* 1978, 49:307–310.

Wolman, B. B., and Money, J. (Eds.) *Handbook of Human Sexuality.* Englewood Cliffs, N.J.: Prentice-Hall, 1980.

5

ADOLESCENT DEVELOPMENT

INTRODUCTION

Our view of adolescence as a commonly experienced stage of development marking the transition from childhood to adulthood is a fairly recent phenomenon. The term "adolescence," meaning "to grow up" or "growing in maturity," was initially used in the first half of the fifteenth century, but was not used to denote a period of development until the eighteenth century. Prior to that time, individuals were assumed to progress directly from childhood into adulthood. Those conflicts that are thought to be the focus of adolescence as we understand it today were not important to most youth. Before the industrial revolution, most children automatically took their parents' occupations, rarely moved far away from home, and usually were isolated from their peers. Only the upper class had time and opportunity to question identity, to associate with peer groups, and to choose a career different from the careers of their parents. Adolescent issues have been identified as early as Aristotle's time – but only for the upper class. In his *Rhetoric*, Aristotle had the following to say about adolescence:

> Young men have strong passions, and tend to gratify them indiscriminately. Of the bodily desires, it is the sexual by which they are most swayed and in which they show absence of self-control. They are changeable and fickle in their desires, which are violent while they last, but quickly over.

With the shift from a primarily agricultural society to an industrial one at the turn of this century, several changes occurred that contributed to adolescence becoming a developmental stage common to all classes. First, the period of formal education was extended; this allowed for greater peer interaction and lengthened the time of financial dependence on parents. Second, increased industrialization gave children greater opportunity to pursue an occupation different from that of their parents. Consequently, in the early 1900s G. Stanley Hall (1904), in association with Freud, described adolescence as a period through which most individuals pass prior to adulthood.

The developmental stage of adolescence involves psychological, sociological, and physiological growth. Adolescence is popularly defined as a period of life that begins with puberty and extends for 8 to 10 years or longer until the person is physically and psychologically mature, ready to assume adult responsibilities and to be self-sufficient because of changes in intellect, attitudes and interests (Cole and Hall 1970; Marlow 1973; Murray and Zentner 1979). Typically this stage occurs from approximately age 11 to age 21. (Puberty refers to the first phase of adolescence when sexual maturation becomes evident.) Unlike earlier developmental stages, the endpoint of adolescence is determined by the completion of psychosocial tasks rather than physiological development. Consequently there is a great deal of individual variability and little agreement among theorists as to age of completion. For example, Kimball and Campbell (1979) stated, "A sign of the successful completion of adolescence is the achievement of satisfactory separation from the family and the ability to live independently on one's own." By such criteria many medical students and other health professionals in training, who are sometimes still financially dependent on parents, would not be considered to have completed adolescence. Freud (1950) viewed the establishment of a primary heterosexual relationship as an endpoint; Erikson (1970) believed the end of adolescence is marked by a complete identity resolution; Friedenberg (1959) believed adolescence is complete when a career choice and a sense of social responsibility is obtained. The stage of adolescence is similar to adult developmental stages in that emphasis is on completion of psychosocial tasks irrespective of chronological age.

Developmental Tasks

The following are issues that are typically resolved during adolescence.

1. Resolution of issues of puberty resulting in a satisfactory body image.
2. Establishment of a firm, positive identity.
3. Establishment of sexual adequacy and intimate relationships.
4. Independence from parents.
5. Commitment to occupational and educational goals.

THE FAMILY

The development of the adolescent occurs within some type of family system. Consequently, developmental issues involving other family members must be assessed in order to accurately view the interplay with the adolescent. For example, parents of adolescents may be at the stage where they are struggling with intimacy issues within their marriage (Kimmel 1974). These conflicts might influence how they view their adolescent's emerging sexuality. Second, the position of the adolescent in the family may also make issues more complex. For example, an adolescent daughter who is the oldest child may be exploring possibilities for a career choice at the same time her mother and father are realizing that they, at age 40 or 50, are at their career peak and may not advance much further. An adolescent boy who is the youngest child may be focusing on career issues at the time his parents are adjusting to retirement.

The overall goal of the family, regardless of specific issues, is to allow the adolescent increasing freedom and responsibility. This involves a process that begins in early adolescence at a time when children are still quite dependent on parents. The young adolescent may flaunt a pseudo-independent image and cause open conflicts with parents. By late adolescence, young people should develop a greater inner sense of independence and autonomy and a more mutually tolerant relationship with parents (Looney, Oldham, and Blotcky 1978).

Some of the following may cause stress between the adolescent and other family members:

1. Differences in appearance, style, and orientation.
2. Parental envy of adolescent freedom and risk-taking (Murray and Zentner 1979).
3. Differences between parents and adolescents in measuring up to one another's demands and often nonverbalized expectations.

4. Difficulties of parents adjusting to the fluctuating needs of adolescents, who at times may be very dependent and at other times very independent.
5. Parental loss of importance and intimacy in the relationship with the adolescent.
6. Mixed messages may increase. For example, an adolescent may protest parental restraints and simultaneously be relieved by them (Murray and Zentner 1979).
7. Adolescent struggles and probing questions may stir up unresolved conflicts in parents regarding, for example, career choice, relationship issues, or sexuality.

PHYSICAL DEVELOPMENT

Growth

With the exception of the first year of life, no other developmental period results in as rapid a rate of growth as adolescence. Females average a growth spurt of 6.35 to 12.7 cm (2 to 5 inches) in a year; males average 7.62 to 15.24 cm (3 to 6 inches) of growth in a year. In addition to sexual development, body mass increases 50 percent, and the individual achieves the final 20–25 percent of linear growth (Smith 1979). The total process of adolescent growth takes 3 years in females and 4 years in males (Tanner 1962).

Individual differences in age of onset of the growth spurt and rapidity of growth are notable. Some adolescents may not have begun pubertal change at an age at which their peers have entirely completed all pubertal events. Usually females begin their growth spurt at age 11 and have completed puberty by age 16, although completing puberty as late as age 21 is not considered abnormal in adolescent females. Males tend to begin growth spurts at age 13 and finish by age 19, but some males may not reach complete adult height until age 25 (Mussen et al. 1979). Two measures indicate growth retardation: The child whose height does not fall within three standard deviations of the mean height for his or her chronological age and the child whose height falls below the third percentile on standard anthropometric charts are both categorized as growth retarded. Earlier recognition of the abnormally growing child may be made by observing the individual's growth velocity (rate of growth in cm per year). Normal children from approximately age 2 to age 12 grow at the rate of 5 cm or more per year (Kogut 1973).

Differences in growth may also occur within the individual (the principle of discontinuity). That is, although every physiological system is growing rapidly, growth occurs unevenly. For example, the skeleton grows faster than supporting muscles, hands and feet become out of proportion to the rest of the body, and large muscles grow faster than small. Psychological consequences of such changes will be discussed later in this chapter.

Differences in growth patterns also occur among cultural groups and races. One study found that Chinese adolescent females from Hong Kong show an earlier height spurt, menarche, and advanced skeletal maturity than do European adolescents (Murray and Zentner 1979). In another study, white girls in Appalachia and Eurasian girls in Hawaii were found to begin puberty later and progress more slowly than their peers in the Midwest (Rauh, Johnson, and Burket 1973). The health professional, therefore, must be careful in using predictive tables in applying norms to adolescents. These norms are only useful if the adolescent comes from the same population as the population on which the data in the table are based.

Besides the skeletal and muscular growth that is easily recognized in the adolescent growth spurt, other systems reach adult development. By age 21, lung capacity matures, red blood cells mass and hemoglobin concentration increases, and the gastrointestinal system reaches adult maturity (Murray and Zentner 1979). Although the heart approximately doubles its weight during adolescence (Freiberg 1979) its rate of growth is slow compared to the rest of the body (Murray and Zentner 1979). This may result in inadequate oxygenation and reports of fatigue. The heart will continue to enlarge until the adolescent reaches age 17 or 18. Systolic blood pressure and pulse rate increase; blood pressure averages 100–120/50–70. Pulse rate averages 60 to 68 beats per minute. Males eventually have a higher systolic pressure and lower pulse rate and basal temperature than females. Hypertension is becoming more common among adolescents, particularly among blacks, the obese, and those with a family history of hypertension (Chinn 1974), and warrants the attention of the health care professional.

Puberty

Factors that are influenced by health care delivery systems have had surprising effects on physical development through adolescence. Better nutrition, particularly more protein and calories in early infancy, as well as an overall improvement in heath and advances in treatment and prevention of debilitating childhood disease has led to what developmental psychologists have called a "secular trend" in puberty. Because of environmental (or secular) effects over the past 200 years, adolescents are growing faster, are becoming larger and stronger, and are reaching adult height at an earlier age. For example, in 1955 a 15-year-old American male was 13.34 cm (5.25 inches) taller and 14.85 kg (33 pounds) heavier than his counterpart in 1870. A medieval knight's armor would only fit the average 10-year-old today. The onset of puberty is also occurring at an increasingly earlier age. Tanner (1962) reported a trend in the lowering of the age of menarche by 3 or 4 months per decade. Thus the average age of menarche in 1860 was 16.5 years; today the average age of menarche for comparable populations is less than 12. Since ovulation occurs 12 to 24 months following menarche, today's average American female is able to conceive by age 14; the average male should be fertile by 15.5 years. Although there are some signs that the secular trend is leveling off, an understanding of this phenomenon is important to the health professional for two reasons. First, it is still conceivable that a daughter will begin menstruating 10 months earlier than her mother did. Parents should be informed of the possibility of earlier onset of puberty, and adolescents should be prepared sooner for the expected changes of puberty. Second, the secular trend has been reversed in populations under deprivation (such as children in concentration camps during World War II) and in individuals with a history of poor diet and health care. For example, menarche is associated with a weight of 47.25 kg (105 pounds); consequently, poor nutrition will slow onset. The health professional working with deprived populations or in countries without living standards similar to those of the United States should alter expectations regarding onset of puberty.

Racial differences also exist in physical development. Although adult statures are about the same, black males and females attain a greater proportion of their adult stature earlier. In addition, because skeletal mass is greater in black people, using white norms could result in bone loss going undetected (Murray and Zentner 1979). Chinese females also tend to show an earlier growth spurt in height, earlier menarche, and earlier skeletal maturity than Europeans (Murray and Zentner 1979).

Physiological Process

Puberty is the period of physiological change during which the male and female sexual organs mature. The onset of puberty is determined by the interaction of gonadal hormones and the hypothalamus. In childhood, until age 8 or 9, there are trace levels of circulating gonadal hormone that are thought to have an inhibitory effect on the hypothalamus (Donovan 1959). Inhibition of the hypothalamus keeps the anterior lobe of the pituitary from secreting gonadotropins that would otherwise evoke secretion of sex hormones in functional amounts. The significant change of puberty is the change of the cells of the hypothalamus so that the trace levels of gonadal hormone are no longer inhibitory. The factors that influence this change in the human brain are not yet completely understood. With the hypothalamus no longer inhibited, neurohumors are produced that stimulate the pituitary gland. The pituitary gland then releases the gonadotropic hormones that stimulate sexual hormone production. This gonadotropin level does not reach the adult "set point" until after mid-adolescence. In the female, there is a late development of the mid-cycle peak in luteinizing hormone (a gonadotropin) production that is necessary for ovulation. Maximum fertility and regular ovulation is probably not achieved until late teens or early twenties (Tanner 1962). In the male, Leydig cells of the testes produce testosterone. In the female, the ovarian follicles produce estradiol. Wolstenhome and O'Connor (1967) suggested that this dramatic increase in hormone production may be related to increased aggressiveness and rapid mood change during adolescence. Although research with adults has demonstrated a relationship between increased dehydroisoandrosterone, a mildly potent androgen, and increased aggressiveness (Wolstenholme and O'Connor 1967) similar research with populations undergoing puberty has been inconclusive.

Simultaneously, as the gonadotropic hormones are released, the adrenal cortex increases the production of androgens. Androgens are the male hormones responsible for producing secondary sex characteristics. Since each individual produces both male and female hormones, the resultant secondary sex characteristics depend upon which hormone is produced in the larger amount. The male physique is produced by androgens, the female physique by estrogens. Growth slows at the end of puberty because both forms of the gonadal hormones eventually repress the pituitary growth hormone (Illig and Prader 1970; Tanner et al. 1971). The stages of sexual development during puberty for males and females are detailed in Tables 5-1 and 5-2.

Psychological Effects

Besides the profound physical effects of puberty, psychological and social reactions occur that may influence self-concept and body image. The health professional's role is important in dealing with the emotional consequences of normal development and the complexities that may result from illness at a time of such personal vulnerability.

Body image is a complex issue for the adolescent. The adolescent must adjust to a new shape and size that may not conform to the ideal body he or she wished for in childhood. Initially the new body is awkward, disproportionate, and clumsy. Hands and feet may be out of proportion to the rest of the body; large muscles grow faster than the small muscles that control fine motor movements (Freiberg 1979). The adolescent's attention is often focused on the body part that is changing. Extreme sensitivity results leading to a distorted self-view. Defects are often overemphasized and become representative of total self-worth. Understandably, concern over body image becomes pervasive and of greater importance to the early adolescent than social or intellectual traits (Mussen et al. 1979). Often the adolescent is deeply concerned about physical attractiveness and is especially vulnerable to real or imagined assaults on bodily integrity. The normally developing adolescent sometimes copes with such concerns by focusing attention on the body surface. Much time is spent in front of mirrors; energy and money is invested in products for body hygiene and grooming, as well as in clothing.

The social network also becomes important in the development of body image. Remarks from peers about appearance have great influence on self-esteem. Adolescents are more likely than other age groups to interpret remarks about appearance ("you look awful") as personality criticisms ("you are awful") (Mussen et al. 1979). This

TABLE 5-1
FEMALE STAGES OF SEXUAL DEVELOPMENT

AGE	STAGES

0-12   I.   Preadolescent. Female pelvic countour evident, breast flat,
             labia majora smooth and minora are poorly developed, hymenal
             opening small or absent, mucous membranes dry and red, vaginal
             cells lack glycogen.
8-13   II. Breasts: Elevation of nipple, small mound beneath areola which
             is enlarging and begins pigmentation. Labia majora become
             thickened, more prominent and wrinkled, labia minora easily
             identified due to increased size along with clitoris, urethral
             opening more prominent, mucous membranes moist and pink, some
             glycogen present in vaginal cells. Ovarian follicles begin
             to develop and uterine growth occurs.
             Hair: First appears on mons and then on labia majora about
             time of menarche, still scanty, soft and straight.
             Skin: Increased activity of sebaceous and merocrine sweat
             glands and initial function of apocrine glands in axilla and
             vulva begin. Growth and remolding of bony pelvis.
9-14   III. Rapid growth peak is passed, menarche most often at this stage
             and invariably follows the peak of growth acceleration.
             Breasts: Areola and nipple further enlarged and pigmentation
             more evident, continued increase in glandular size. Labia
             minora well developed and vaginal cells have increased glycogen
             content, mucous membranes increasingly more pale, clitoris
             enlarges, vaginal secretion commences.
             Hair: In pubic region thicker, coarser, often curly (con-
             siderable normal variation including a few girls with early
             stage II at menarche).
             Skin: Further increased activity of sebaceous and sweat glands
             with beginning of acne in some girls, adult body odor.
12-15   IV. Breasts: Projection of areola above breast plan and areolar
             glands apparent (this development is absent in about 20% of
             normal girls). Glands easily palpable.
             Labia: Both majora and minora assume adult structure, glycogen
             content of vaginal cells begins cyclic characteristics.
             Hair in pubic area more abundant, axillary hair present (rarely
             present at stage II, not uncommonly present at stage III).
12-17   V.   Breasts: Mature histologic morphology, nipple enlarged and
             erect, areolar glands well developed, globular shape.
             Hair in pubic area more abundant and may spread to thighs (in
             about 10% of women it assumes "male" distribution with extension
             toward umbilicus). Facial hair increases often in form of
             slight mustache.
             Skin: Increased sebaceous gland activity and increased severity
             of acne if present before.
             Full reproductive function not attained until 12-24 months after
             menarche.

Sources: Freiberg (1979); Kogut (1973); Tanner (1962); Wilkins (1965).

CHAPTER 5

TABLE 5-2
MALE STAGES OF SEXUAL DEVELOPMENT

AGE		STAGES

0-14	I.	Preadolescent.
10-14	II.	Increasing size of testes and penis is evident (testicle length reaches 2.0 cm or more). Scrotum integument is thinner and assumes an increased pendulous appearance. Hair: First appearance of pubic hair in area at base of penis. Skin: Increased activity of sebaceous and apocrine sweat glands and initial function of apocrine glands on axilla and scrotal area begins.
11-15	III.	Rapid growth peak is passed, nocturnal emissions begin. Testes and penis: Further increase in size and pigmentation apparent. Leydig cells (interstitial) first appear at stage II, are now prominent in testes. Hair: In pubic area more abundant and present on scrotum, still scanty and fine textured, axillary hair begins. Breasts: Button-type hypertrophy in 70% of boys at stages II and III. Larynx: Changes in voice due to laryngeal growth begins. Skin: Increasing activity of sebaceous and sweat glands with beginning of acne, adult body odor.
12-16	IV.	Testes: Further increase in size, length 4.0 cm. or greater, increase in size of penis greatest at stages III and IV. Hair: Pubic hair thicker and coarser and in most ascends toward umbilicus in typical male pattern, axillary hair increases, facial hair increases over lip and upper cheeks. Larynx: Voice deepens. Skin: Increasing pigmentation of scrotum and penis, acne often more severe. Breasts: Previous hypertrophy decreased or absent.
13-17	V.	Testes: Length greater than 4.5 cm. Hair: Pubic hair thick, curly, heavily pigmented, extends to thighs and toward umbilicus. Adult distribution and increase in body hair (chest, shoulders, thighs, etc.) continues for more than 10 years. Baldness, if present, may begin. Skin: Acne may persist and increase. Larynx: Adult character of voice.

Sources: Freiberg (1979); Kogut (1973); Tanner (1962); Wilkins (1965).

social sensitivity leads to an interesting form of narcissism. That is, adolescents spend time observing others observing them. They may, at the same time, be both flamboyant and shy. It is not uncommon for an adolescent to wear a dramatically unusual piece of clothing that attracts attention and is, at the same time, quite bulky and camouflages body contour. Health professionals are often confused by the adolescent who is seductively dressed yet very shy about disrobing.

These issues about body image become more complex for the

adolescent with health problems. If the adolescent does have a disability or defect, peers and adults may react with fear, pity, revulsion, or curiosity. The adolescent may retain and later reflect these impressions because they occur at a stage of identity formation. Vulnerability about assaults on bodily integrity is intensified at this age. Illness, loss of function, surgery, and scarring may engender intense fear and may have a strong impact on self-concept. Although all patients of various ages have similar concerns, adolescence is the stage in which concerns may be more intense, confusion about body image and function may be greatest, and self-image most vulnerable.

In addition to the general concerns of adolescents about body image, specific pubertal changes have psychological consequences. Among those that warrant the special attention of the health care professional are female menstruation and breast development in both females and males.

Menstruation. Menstruation has different significance in various cultures. For example, American Indians attributed mystical powers to the woman during her menstrual period and isolated her from the tribe. Menarche is typically experienced in our culture as affectively charged even though no formal customs mark it and no obvious change in social status occurs. Unfortunately, adolescents are often unprepared for its occurrence. A study of 103 upper-class women found that 21 percent had no advance preparation, and many of these reported fear of internal bleeding and death. Of those who had advance warning, 75 percent reported being fearful or worried (Mussen, Conger, and Kagan 1974). In another study, only 15 percent of mothers showed pleasure when told that their daughters had begun menstruating (Mussen, Conger, and Kagan 1974). Often menses is perceived as an excretory function (Murray and Zentner 1979). Adolescents also make assumptions about the effects of strenuous exercise on menstruation and, conversely, are concerned that menstruation will inhibit athletic performance. Such assumptions have been found to be unwarranted (Shaffer 1973) and may be corrected by the health professional.

Breast Development. Breast development may cause concern among males and females. Enlargement of the breasts and rounding of the contours of the hips are the first discernible pubertal change in females. By the time of menarche, the small budding breasts have progressively enlarged to assume a conical shape. The mature or rounded form gradually develops during the next 2 to 4 years (Tanner

1962). The female adolescent may express concern to the health professional regarding the size or shape of her breasts; typically this concern reflects our cultural overemphasis on appearance or peer-group influences. She may also express concern over unevenness in development at which point the health professional may explain that both breasts are likely to be the same size when she is fully mature (Shaffer 1973).

Some hypertrophy of the breasts occurs in about 70 percent of male adolescents (Lowrey 1978). The peak incidence is between ages 14 and 15, after the genitalia have begun to grow and pubic hair has appeared. As adolescence advances, this gynecomastia gradually disappears, but it may persist for as long as 2 years, causing concern for the adolescent boy. Some degree of tenderness, particularly following even minor trauma, is also common. As in females, asymmetric enlargement may be present.

Early and Late Maturation

Early and late development may have different consequences at different times during adolescence. During early adolescence, both social advantages and disadvantages may result. For example, an early developing male tends to have increased social status because he is taller, stronger, and appears more mature than his peers. An early developing female, however, may be socially disadvantaged because she is taller and larger than her peers (Gross and Duke 1980). But if one takes into account the adolescent's ability to cope with such significant physical changes, the female's accelerated social maturity and self-concept would place her at an advantage over her male peer in coping with early development.

Research suggests that correlations exist betwen maturation and behavior, but that they may differ among cohorts and between males and females (Mussen, Conger, and Kagan 1974). A survey study, using data from the National Center for Health Statistics, examined correlations between behavioral attributes and maturation assessed using stages developed by Tanner's (1962) physiological research. Early and later developers were identified by a matrix using the upper and lower 20 percent of the distribution of Tanner stages for each age and sex. Significant results were found in relation to educational characteristics and body image. Based on adolescent and parental educational aspirations and expectations, teachers' reports, and test scores, late maturing males appeared to be educationally disadvantaged compared to medium and early maturers. Regarding body image, early maturing boys and girls reported themselves as thinner than their peers. In an interesting sex difference, early maturing boys reported satisfaction with their weight whereas early maturing girls expressed dissatisfaction (Gross and Duke 1980).

When dealing with the early or late maturing adolescent, the health professional should encourage the expression of individual concerns and may reassure and educate. The health professional may be helpful in clarifying individual concerns, such as when the adolescent might expect to reach full adult height.

COGNITIVE DEVELOPMENT

Cognitive development during adolescence interacts with all other aspects of development during this period: self-identity, parental relations, risk-taking behavior, and sexuality. Of continuing concern to the health professional is the way in which the child's level of cognitive maturity determines his or her understanding of disease, medical procedures, and consequences of interventions.

Piaget's last phrase of cognitive development, the potential for formal operations, is possible for the first time during adolescence. This phase represents the highest level of intellectual functioning. According to Piaget, the most sophisticated level of operations that the child can perform prior to adolescence is concrete operations. A child with the ability to perform concrete operations can deal with classifications, serialization, and one-to-one correspondence. By comparison, adolescents in the phase of formal operations are far more capable. The adolescent:

1. Is able to recognize new kinds of logical relationships between classes or between and among several different properties (without actual objects) on the abstract level.
2. Also becomes proficient at combination analysis—being able to see all the possible variations of a problem or separating out all the possible variables and then testing them systematically.
3. Is able to focus on the process of problem solving rather than just on content. This means the adolescent is capable of using logic and can systematically critique an argument.
4. Can use hypothetical-deductive reasoning in problem solving.

119

Such reasoning involves generating a set of hypotheses and then testing each one to deduce the correct answer(s). Solutions that are derived may be real (what can be seen, felt, and experienced) and may also encompass abstract "what if" solutions. In short, all possible variations can be considered (Flavell 1977).

These capabilities result in an individual who can use available information to entertain theories and look for supporting facts, consider alternate solutions to problems, project his thinking into the future, and categorize thoughts into usable forms. The adolescent can solve hypothetical, mental, and verbal problems; use scientific reasoning; and can deal with the past, present, and future. In early adolescence, the individual may find it gratifying to play with the ability to abstract, "like a new toy instead of a practical and useful tool" (Looney, Oldham, and Blotcky 1978). Initially this capacity for abstract thinking is of little help to the young adolescent in understanding his or her own behavior. Often theories are oversimplified and lack originality.

As the individual progresses through adolescence, introspection typically increases. For the first time, the person is able to conceptualize the self in abstract terms, as if he or she were a spectator. Adolescents imagine themselves in other roles, different settings, and with new values. In part, this new capability results in an egocentrism often noted by adults. Adolescents are able to see all the realms of possibility but sometimes fail to distinguish between their own conceptualizations and those of the rest of society. They fail to see that others may not like or want what they want. This egocentricity also takes the form of believing that everyone is extremely concerned with the adolescent's appearance and behavior. Often adolescents feel that others are as preoccupied with appearance as they are. This self-involvement can easily turn into self-criticism. When adolescents find themselves lacking in some way, they often believe the whole world can see the same deficiency. Personal programs of self-improvement may begin with intensity but be hindered by excessive self-criticism. Eventually these feelings of omnipotence, near-genius insightfulness, absolute uniqueness, and extreme self-criticism become hypotheses to be cognitively tested. The consequence of the testing process is that adolescents begin to realize that the world is not focused on them. By late adolescence, the individual neither overestimates nor devalues this capacity for abstract thought but uses this capacity to gain insight into his or her own situation.

In addition to these ways in which cognitive development influences self-concept, these new intellectual capabilities affect the adolescent's relationship with family and other social networks. The adolescent is able to use these new abilities to abstractly construct an ideal family or an ideal hospital setting. When these ideals are compared with reality, the adult way of constructing society is often found lacking. Idealism may be intense, yet often the adolescent has difficulty implementing and dealing with reality. Interaction of this idealism with narcissism may result in seemingly callous criticism of staff, parents, or hospital functions. This behavior may often lead to the conflicts that have been collectively labeled the generation gap.

In addition, these new intellectual capabilities allow adolescents to use more sophisticated coping strategies in dealing with stress. They are capable of intellectualizing illness by separating facts from emotion. In such cases, individuals often show a marked interest in the minute details associated with the illness.

Critique of Piaget

In criticism of Piaget, Mussen (1973) cited studies that show a lack of formal-operations thought in many adults in the United States and Europe. He argued that those individuals who develop formal operations have had greater opportunities to learn vocabularies with abstract words, to use concrete props, to learn about relationships, and were encouraged to order concepts. In addition, even among those individuals with the capacity for formal operations, a complex picture emerges. Wilson (1978) demonstrated, for example, that adolescents who are capable of abstraction in making moral decisions about neutral issues revert to concrete thinking when faced with making similar decisions in the more ambivalent and anxiety-producing area of sexuality.

Consequently, the health professional needs to assess individual cognitive development when working with adolescent patients. The ability to abstract is a significant element of maturity; it is important in making reasoned decisions about health care and giving informed consent (Hofman 1980). Concrete thinkers may encounter difficulty in appreciating the consequences of their actions in terms of the future. For example, a young adolescent smoker may be capable of perceiving the adverse effects of cigarettes as reflected in his impaired athletic ability or financial demands, but not in terms of increased risk of pulmonary or cardiovascular disease during middle age (Hofman 1980).

IDENTITY FORMATION

The development of a unique and consistent sense of identity has long been regarded as a necessary goal for the stage of adolescence. Much of Erikson's writings on adolescence involve the conflict of identity formation versus identity diffusion. An adaptive resolution of the conflict results in identity formation. Maladaption, or identity diffusion, leads to a sense of instability in the midst of many confusing intrinsic and social demands. In identifying the goals of adolescence, Erikson (1974, pp. 21–22) stated, "A strong sense of identity means a sense of being at one with oneself as one grows and develops . . . to see oneself as a distinctive individual, in some respect like no other person, even though one may share many motives, values and interests with others." Feelings of self-consistency, seeing your needs and capabilities as part of a coherent whole, and considering even negative aspects of your personality to be part of yourself are all components of this sense of identity.

The development of identity involves both an introspective process and an interaction with society that results in an adult social role. The introspective process includes, as previously discussed, the development of a body image and cognitive development. In addition, other factors will be discussed that contribute to the introspective process of identity formation. These include the creation of a self-concept through modeling or identification, establishing independence, and the creation of a sex-role identity. Career choice, another component of identity, is primarily a concern of the young adult.

Process of Identity Formation

As individuals progress through adolescence, they move from early stages of identity confusion to a solid sense of identity. This usually occurs by late adolescence or early adulthood. The early adolescent, who has not yet developed a strong sense of identity, may show traits similar to those that characterize identity diffusion as described by Erikson. An individual might manifest identity diffusion in a number of ways. Such an individual may be a wanderer who lacks future goals and direction as well as intimate relationships; may overidentify with a public figure or social cause in a reactive, stereotyped manner; or may play several roles that shift from one situation to another (Erikson 1974). Although the early adolescent and the more psychopathological individual suffering from identity diffusion appear to be similar, their differences are significant. Identity diffusion tends to be characterological and relatively unchanging whereas the identity confusion of early adolescence eventually matures into a solid sense of self.

Through this process of identity formation, the adolescent becomes more effective in integrating three types of identity: (1) personal or real identity—what I believe myself to be, (2) ideal identity—what I would like to be, and (3) social identity—what I would like others to think I am (Murray and Zentner 1979). Part of this integration occurs through the process of identification. Identification may be defined as admiring, imitating, and sympathizing with high-status individuals—parents, teachers, siblings, or peers—in order to create a personal set of values and behaviors. The health professional who has had positive interactions with an adolescent may become the object of such identification. This can result in an idealistic, sometimes unrealistic view of the professional by the adolescent.

Adolescents often identify with the parent of the same sex. Heilbrun (1970) found that adolescent boys with nurturant fathers perceived themselves as having greater role consistency than did sons of less nurturant men. They saw themselves as responding in consistent, similar ways to parents, friends, employers, casual acquaintances, and members of the opposite sex in a variety of situations. Adolescent girls who scored high in identification with their mothers tended to perceive themselves positively—as "calm, reasonable, reserved, self-controlled, confident, and wise." In contrast, girls who scored low in identification tended to view themselves as "changeable, impulsive, rebellious, restless, dramatic, touchy and tactless" (Block and Turula 1963).

Sex-Role Identity. Like other aspects of identity formation—body image and cognitive development—sex-role identity formation is greatly influenced by parental figures and begins in early childhood

123

(Lynn 1974; Kagan 1979; Bem 1974). Sex-role identity can be defined as the degree to which an individual regards himself or herself as masculine or feminine.

The importance of sex-role identity in predicting behavior in adolescence has recently been questioned in the literature. A weakness in this area involves the definition of sex-role identity. In the past, observers assumed that masculinity and femininity were bipolar ends of a single continuum. A person had to be either masculine or feminine but not both. This sex-role dichotomy is limited in two ways. First, it does not account for individuals who may be androgynous—that is, who display both masculine and feminine behaviors. Such individuals may be instrumental and expressive, mechanical and nurturing, depending on the situation. Second, it does not account for the possibility that individuals who are strongly sex-typed might be seriously limited in the range of behaviors available to them. Unfortunately, most recent research studying the behavioral correlates of androgyny has used adult populations.

Research on sex-role identity in adolescence has primarily focused on peer relationships among males and achievement issues among females. Mussen and colleagues (1979) stated that male sex-role identity has complex effects during adolescence. They reported that adolescents with traditional, highly masculine interests are typically more self-confident than boys with relatively feminine interests. Masculine boys tend to be more carefree, contented, relaxed, and exuberant. They tend to feel happier, calmer, and smoother in social interactions than do less masculine boys. However, when the highly masculine boys reach young adulthood, they may suffer decreases in self-confidence and self-acceptance. Less masculine boys tend to change in a favorable direction and feel more positive about themselves as they grow older. One possible explanation for this may be that masculine traits are highly rewarded in the culture of the adolescent peer group but are less adaptive in adult society.

Research on sex identity in female adolescents has looked at factors that affect achievement. Studies that have evolved since Horner's (1972) early work on women's fears of success emphasize that achievement behavior is often considered gender-role inappropriate for females as they grow older (Tresemer 1977). This explains findings, for example, that although females enter college with better achievement records than do men (Astin et al. 1974), college women nevertheless set lower educational and vocational goals for themselves (Davis 1964; Howe and Ahlum 1973).

It is also important to consider, however, the effects of inconsistencies in academic counseling, test anxiety, and methodological problems in research design (Billingham 1978) that have not yet been systematically addressed in the literature.

Independence. One of the major goals involved in becoming an adult in our society is to establish a sense of independence from the family of origin (Freud 1950). An individual cannot complete identity formation without some resolution of dependence-independence issues involving the family. This task is quite complex. For the adolescent, motivations and rewards are often equally strong for independent and dependent behaviors. In addition, the adolescent's bids for independence may trigger difficulties for parental figures, such as anxiety about growing older, changing roles, and questions of separation and intimacy in the marital relationship. Unfortunately, our society does not provide many guidelines, as do other cultures, to help adolescents and parents separate. Many cultures provide rituals for passage into adulthood that serve to answer questions of when do children become adults and how independent they should be (Muuss 1975). In our culture some rites of passage do exist, although they vary greatly in the guidelines they provide: Voting age, being eligible for military draft, public drinking privileges, and independence in decisions to marry are examples. In addition, certain subgroups have rites of independence, such as bar mitzvahs and bas mitzvahs in the Jewish religion and renaming ceremonies among some American Indians. The adolescent may also identify his or her own personal rite of passage into independence: first job, going to college, menarche, first shave, or loss of virginity.

The process of developing independence often begins with increased separation from parental figures. The adolescent may be ambivalent toward independence. The desire for independence may coexist with a reluctance to give up the security of childhood; the adolescent desires to try out new powers and skills while fearing the loneliness of being on his or her own. The contradictory behaviors that may result from this ambivalence may be intensified by the stress of hospitalization. This move toward independence may also result in moodiness and mourning over the "death" of relationships and loss of

125

the child role. Increased contact and closeness with peers is often used for comfort and approval. Friedman and Sarles (1980) stated that such moodiness and preoccupation with peers is often threatening to parents. Adults may be hurt and baffled by the adolescent's unpredictable, hostile, or moody behavior and may react in a counterpunitive style that results in a downward spiral of negative interactions. The health professional may have to make a rough determination of whether conflicts between the adolescent and his or her family are due to normal bids for independence or to more pathological struggles that interfere with medical care and require a psychological or psychiatric referral.

Like other aspects of development, the development of independence occurs within a family system. That system has a history of dealing with conflicts, making decisions, and relating to independence in its members. Consequently, a diagnosis involving pathological rebelliousness versus more typical striving for independence should begin with an understanding of the family system. Commenting on a study of several thousand American and Danish adolescents and their parents, Lesser and Kandel (1969, p. 307) noted a similarity of independence training in the two countries:

> In both countries, feelings of independence were enhanced when parents had few rules, and when they were democratic and engaged the child actively in the decision-making process. Furthermore, feelings of independence from parents in both countries, far from leading to rebelliousness, are associated with closeness to parents and positive attitudes toward them.

Additional literature supports Lesser and Kandel's conclusions that ostensible attitudes of parental figures are not enough to insure effective independence training. In this regard, Blum (1972) found that drug abuse and other forms of socially deviant behavior occurred most frequently among middle-class adolescents whose parents outwardly expressed values of individuality, independence, and the need for egalitarianism in the family, but who were actually using these proclaimed values to avoid parental responsibility. These parents, despite statements about togetherness, spent less time in family activities with their children, enjoyed their company less, and were less able to handle family problems than were more traditional parents of low-drug-risk adolescents.

In viewing the individual adolescent separate from the family, the health professional often needs to assess the degree of conflict and areas of conflict. Mussen and colleagues (1979) reported that girls in our culture often experience fewer and less stressful conflicts over the development of independence than do boys. Girls are more likely than boys to consider their parent's rules as fair, right, or lenient. Offer (1969) conducted a longitudinal study to assess behavioral patterns and coping skills of 103 high-school males who were identified as model adolescents. Several years of follow-up study revealed that rebellious behavior normatively occurred only in early adolescence and was typically manifested as minor disagreements with authority figures over matters of music, dress, and curfew. In contrast, Looney and colleagues (1978) cited clinical studies that demonstrate that adolescent psychiatric patients showed significantly more symptoms involving delinquent behavior, thought disorder, and personality disturbance than did nonpatient controls. This literature indicates that only mild forms of anxiety and depression disturb normal adolescence. Follow-up studies of adolescent psychiatric patients and epidemiologic studies by Weiner and Del Gaudio (1976) and by Looney and Gunderson (1978) suggest that their symptom patterns persist and become more clearly differentiated over time.

Clearly there are several issues regarding adolescent independence that affect health care treatment. The professional must distinguish between pathological family conflict and the normal struggles that arise from strivings for independence. The health professional must also know how to respond to the contradictory behavior of adolescents. In addition, independence issues may arise in relation to negotiating treatment, responsibility for taking medications, and confidentiality from parental figures. These issues will be discussed in the section on health considerations.

ADOLESCENT SEXUALITY

Sexual awareness begins in early infancy with impressions of sensuality (Kolodny, Masters, and Johnson 1979) and develops within the social network. By adolescence, the individual must adjust to pubertal changes, develop a sexual identity, and make decisions regarding sexual behavior. Much of what has already been discussed in relation to pubertal changes, body image, and sex-role identity contributes to these processes. In addition to these topics, the health professional must be aware of the prevalence of different sexual behaviors among adolescents, the attitudes of adolescents toward sexual behaviors, their sources of information, dating patterns, and issues involving homosexuality.

Sexual Behavior

Recent surveys have found that adolescents are becoming more sexually active at a younger age. Zelnik and Kantner (1978) indicated that nearly 50 percent of the nation's 10.3 million young women from ages 15 to 19 have had premarital sex. This percentage has nearly doubled since they began their survey in 1971. In addition, according to another national survey, 2 million children, aged 17 and under, are involved in prostitution and pornography. The House Select Committee on Population reported that more than one million adolescent females become pregnant every year—approximately one-third of whom have abortions. The same source found that of the 600,000 adolescents who gave birth in 1977, 250,000 were 17 years old or younger and 13,000 were under the age of 15. Of all females aged 15 in 1973, 40 percent became pregnant at least once before they reached age 20. In the past 18 years, out-of-wedlock births to adolescents have more than doubled. Pregnancy is the single most common cause of school dropout among girls; nearly 70 percent of pregnant students fail to complete high school. Considering these data, it is not surprising to find that approximately 80 percent of the 5 million sexually active adolescents in this country fail to use birth control because of unwillingness, ignorance, or the unavailability of contraceptive devices.

These data clearly indicate that the health professional cannot make assumptions about the sexual behavior of adolescent patients. Studies that indicate the trend over the past 25 years toward more and earlier sexual activity among adolescents have found no discrepancies between adolescent male and female behavior (Jessor and Jessor 1975). Chronological age, however, does not determine sexual behavior. Relevant influences from socioeconomic, cultural, and religious backgrounds contribute to decisions regarding sexual behavior. Although half of adolescent males and females reported that initial coitus was not pleasurable (Froese 1975), physical pleasure is one of the reasons given for deciding to remain sexually active. Other reasons reported were means of communication, search for new experience, index of personal maturity, conformity to peers, challenge to parents or society, reward or punishment, escape from loneliness, and escape from other pressures (Sorenson 1973). When adolescents were motivated primarily by negative forces—to challenge parents, for example—the potential for adverse effects were greater in most circumstances (Sorenson 1973). However, most adolescents report that a sense of love is important in a relationship for sex to occur and that most sexual activity occurs within the context of one primary relationship (Mussen et al. 1979).

Equally important are the reasons given by adolescents for deciding to refrain from coital activity. Kolodny and colleagues (1979) reported the following reasons: fear of pregnancy or venereal disease, not being in love, wishing to preserve later options, self-perception of lack of psychological readiness, lack of opportunity, and religious, cultural, or personal values. The adolescent who chooses to refrain from intercourse does not typically refrain from all sexual activity. The most common form of sexual outlet for both sexes during adolescence is masturbation (Murray and Zentner 1979).

Despite myths and psychiatric literature warning that sexual behavior by adolescents may disrupt ego development and psychological maturation (Mathis 1976), cross-cultural evidence and clinical acumen indicate that harmful psychological effects do not generally ensue from responsible adolescent sexual relationships or from casual sexual activity that is uncoercive as long as adequate contraceptive practices are followed (Kolodny, Masters, and Johnson 1979).

Sexual Dysfunction

Unfortunately, sexual dysfunction among adolescents has not been studied systematically. Those symptoms that require prompt, careful evaluation and treatment are dyspareunia (pain with intercourse) and vaginismus (involuntary constriction of outer third of the vagina during attempts at vaginal penetration) (Kolodny, Masters, and Johnson 1979). Unfortunately we cannot infer from adult sexual dysfunction literature how to treat early ejaculation or nonorganismic disorders in adolescents. Both of these problems could lead to other difficulties of poor self-esteem, depression, and avoidance of sexual activity. Kolodny and colleagues (1979, p. 94) reported that a "fairly substantial number of cases in which sexual difficulties are present during adolescence may reflect inexperience, lack of knowledge, anxiety, and psychological immaturity."

Attitudes and Information Sources

Renshaw (1978) recently reported that adolescents were "sexual illiterates." Only 12 percent of parents talked to their children about sex and these talks were limited to the "origins of babies and menstruation." Families of physicians and ministers were even more limited in that only 2.6 percent of these parents talked with their children about sex. It appears that adolescents seek different sources for different information: abortion – written literature; venereal disease – school; menstruation – mother; homosexuality, intercourse, and masturbation – peers. Therefore, the reliability of the information varies with the source.

Much of the problem of assimilation of information lies with attitudinal differences. A study cited by Mussen and colleagues (1979) found that parents more likely than adolescents tend to (1) disapprove of sex education, (2) want to limit birth-control information and availability of devices, (3) disapprove of premarital sex, and (4) are more concerned with prevailing social codes and less concerned with relationships. Paradoxically, adolescents who were virgins approved of premarital sex, whereas parents who had engaged in premarital sex themselves disapproved of it for others. Only 36 percent of adolescents had the same attitudes as their parents regarding sexual issues. However, most felt that they had relationships with their parents involving mutual respect as long as the discrepancies in attitudes were not too great.

Among adolescents attitudes vary. Young adolescents are more conservative than older adolescents; fewer 13- to 15-year-olds endorsed premarital intercourse than did 16- to 19-year-olds. Females as a group are more likely to view sex in terms of a larger relationship than are males. Economically privileged, college-bound adolescents, as well as those from the East and West coasts, tend to be more liberal (Mussen et al. 1979). It is important to note, however, that adolescents often have more flexible, accepting attitudes toward the behavior of others than toward the standards they set for themselves. Therefore, we cannot assume that expressions of belief are equivalent to actual behavior. This is related, in part, to a shift in attitude among adolescents about what should be viewed as private and not of public concern. Adolescents, in a study cited by Mussen and colleagues (1979), stated that the following should be decided by individuals and were not public moral issues: premarital sex, interracial relationships, consenting homosexual relationships, abortion, and children outside of marriage. Seventy-five percent of the adolescents focused more on the relationship than on behaviors per se.

Dating Patterns

Popular opinion and scientific literature consider a high level of sexual development to be conducive to dating. A study by Gross and Duke (1980), controlling for social class, examined the interrelationships among dating, sexual development, and age. It was found that age was the primary predictor for dating and that sexual development hardly related to dating after age was taken into account. This is an example of a behavior for which the impact of social expectations regarding appropriate age is more influential than biological development.

At first the emphasis in dating is on commonly shared activities, followed by increased intimacy with a focus on a close, sharing relationship. Dating may start with groups of couples, move to double dates, and finally to single couples (Murray and Zentner 1979). However, not all adolescents assume this dating pattern. Some begin to date one person in early adolescence and continue this relationship until marriage. Others do not date until young adulthood.

Homosexual Activities

Prior to any discussion of homosexuality, a conformity of definition is required. The term homosexuality may refer to any of the following: (1) erotic arousal by a person of the same sex regardless of whether there is physical contact, (2) sexual contact with a person of the same sex regardless of whether there is erotic arousal, and (3) arousal to orgasm by physical contacts with individuals of the same sex. It is best to clarify with the patient precisely what is meant.

Diepold and Young (1979) reviewed the literature on adolescent homosexuality. They cited the work of DeLora and Warren who found that of adolescents who report homosexual experiences, the majority of males had their first experience when they were 11 to 12 years old, the majority of females when they were 6 to 10 years old. As males approached late adolescence the likelihood of their having a homosexual experience increased. By the end of adolescence, 20 percent of adolescent males had had at least one homosexual contact that resulted in orgasm. For females, the likelihood of contacts does not increase with age. By the end of adolescence, less than 10 percent of adolescent females had had a homosexual experience. Typically, homosexual experiences during adolescence are transitory and do not lead to a preference for homosexuality in adulthood. The principle danger for the adolescent is in a social stigma, more likely from adults than peers. DeLora and Warren reported that adolescents themselves tend to be tolerant of homosexual activity as long as participants are willing and express concern for the total person rather than just sexual behavior.

HEALTH CARE CONSIDERATIONS

The adolescent is an individual who is struggling to become independent from the family, who is concerned about physical normalcy because of rapid pubertal changes, and who is, very likely, sexually active. All of these characteristics contribute to complex medical management problems that are rarely present in relationships with younger children. This section will review ways to establish good medical practice with this age group. In addition, specific areas relevant to adolescents will be covered: nutritional needs, adolescent pregnancy, adolescent diseases, and dealing with death.

Medical Management

In order to provide good medical care for an adolescent, the health professional needs to be well informed. Adolescents only give information to authority figures with whom they have confidential, trusting relationships. This kind of relationship is sometimes difficult to achieve. First, adolescents are sporadic and disorderly in seeking medical care. At this stage of personality development, they feel invincible and grandiose, never likely to get sick or hurt, and not in need of regular medical examinations. Concerns about the normalcy of their bodies may cause them to ignore conditions or wait too long to find help, and they will typically only seek medical care during a crisis. For example, Wilson (1978) pointed out that adolescent females are twice as likely as older women to wait until they are more than 12 weeks pregnant before making their first appointment to obtain an abortion. This tendency to delay has the largest single effect on risk to adolescents for complications and death from abortions (Zelnik and Kantner 1974). Second, because of the rapid flux of symptoms and needs in adolescents, the presenting problem may not be the real concern. An adolescent may go to a clinic to discuss an earache and end up talking about sexual problems. Often the individual will present a noncontroversial complaint to gain access to the health professional and will only disclose the real concern after mutual trust has been established. Finally, because adolescents are involved in establishing independence from the family and in developing an autonomous sense of self, they feel much ambivalence about seeking professional help. The health professional may be a source of independent information but still represents the parent-age personality. Often this poses a problem of style in relating for the health professional. Neither overfamiliarity and adolescent slang nor aloofness and moralizing are well received. Most success is gained through conveying respect, interest, and willingness to listen.

Initial Interview. The initial interview proves to be a critical time for establishing a good relationship. Three goals of this first contact are: to begin to establish mutual respect, trust, and rapport; to initiate medical procedures that are deemed essential; and to formulate tentative impressions about the adolescent's general state of psychological functioning. Following are several recommendations, based on a collection of research (Billingham 1981; Hofman 1980; Looney, Oldham, and Blotcky 1978):

1. See the adolescent alone, first, before talking with parents. This encourages an autonomous and responsible alliance between the adolescent and health professional. It also counteracts the adolescent's frequent feeling of being forced to seek medical care by an outside authority.
2. As a health professional, you should define your role as that of the adolescent's advocate and care provider, not a representative of the parents. In this context the adolescent may ask any question and pursue any topic.
3. Stress the confidentiality of the relationship. Only if the adolescent reveals self-destructive behavior will the caretaker who is responsible for his or her welfare be informed, and

then only after talking with the adolescent first and only with the adolescent present.

4. Let the adolescent know what information you have been given from the referral source, having previously informed the referring person of this procedure. This prevents confusion and mistrust about what each of you knows about the other.

Issues Involving Parents. In reviewing issues of adolescent independence, it is clear that parents, as well as the adolescents, are ambivalent about separating from their children. In the past, they have been the persons primarily responsible for the child's health. Consequently, an understanding must be reached with parents to allow their adolescents to manage their own health care affairs. Wilson (1978) found that the use of birth control increased dramatically if the adolescent female felt that her relationship with her physician was confidential from her parents. Lett, Cuskey, and Rudd (in press) found that those adolescents who made their own appointments were significantly more compliant in taking medications than those adolescents whose caretakers arranged appointments. Smith (1979) found that parents will frequently misattribute symptoms of emotional upset in their adolescents to organic causes and will seek tests and physical examinations for hypoglycemia or mononucleosis. Therefore, if the focus of treatment is based on the caretaker's views, real sources of upset to the adolescent may be overlooked. Finally, in relation to the role of parents, health professionals should understand the extent of the "mature minor" doctrine in their particular areas of the country (Hofman 1980). In some states, adolescents may receive medical treatment in a variety of circumstances, particularly for venereal disease and contraception, solely on their own consent.

Once a trusting relationship is established with an adolescent, the health professional will be able to make assessments about conflict areas that may require additional attention or psychological referral. Table 5-3 presents questions that the health professional may consider in making such assessments.

Nutritional Needs

During this time of accelerated physical development, the body's metabolic rate increases and, accordingly, nutritional needs increase.

At no other time in development does the male have such great nutritional needs. The adolescent female's requirements are equalled or surpassed only during pregnancy and lactation (Chinn 1974). Even after the obvious period of accelerated growth has ended, nutritional intake must be adequate for the muscle development and bone mineralization that continues. This means that adolescent females require approximately 2,200 to 2,400 calories daily and males need about 3,000. Nutrient deficiencies that are most common for this age group are deficiencies of calcium and iron. Protein deficiency also frequently accompanies iron deficiency. Deficiencies and poor diet are especially of consequence for the pregnant adolescent. Not only will poor diet interfere with her growth requirements, but it will also cause detrimental prenatal effects (see Chapter 2).

Several social and psychological factors influence adolescent diet. Because adolescents are socially active, meals at home are often skipped. When they do eat, they will likely eat junk food at a social gathering, under the scrutiny of friends. Problems with inaccurate body image sometimes result in severe dieting. Often adolescents who are involved with sports will counter peer pressure and maintain a good diet for immediate rewards. Promises of long-term good health have little influence on this age group.

Two eating disorders of which the health professional should be aware are obesity and anorexia nervosa. The normal proportion of adipose tissue (fat) in men is 12 to 18 percent. In women it is 18 to 24 percent. An obese individual has an additional 20 percent of body weight consisting of fat. Obesity in adolescents threatens health and results in poor self-concept. Treatment techniques and issues are reviewed by Gordon (1982). Anorexia nervosa is severe weight loss without the presence of a disease. It is self-induced and mostly occurs in female adolescents. This disorder represents severe psychopathology and requires special consultation. In some cases it has been fatal.

Specific Health Problems

Adolescents seek medical help for accidents, diseases, drug and alcohol abuse, and pregnancy. Head and spinal cord injuries, skeletal injuries, abrasions, and burns often result from automobile or sports-related accidents. Incomplete skeletal development, poor coordination, impulsivity, and unrealistic ideas of physical ability

TABLE 5-3
ADOLESCENT ASSESSMENT

FAMILY

1. General family conflict - Is there conflict between parents? Alcoholism, chronic illness, drug abuse, or violence in the family?

2. Can the adolescent discuss problems and establish a relationship with one or both parents? When was the last time they talked? What events are shared?

3. Issues of personal power - Where does he/she acquire money? Are the restrictions of freedom appropriate for the age and stage of development? What are the responsibilities in the home and out? How are decisions which affect the adolescent made?

4. Is there a comfortable separation from the parents? Does the adolescent have a social life separate from parents? Is dating allowed? Do parents approve of friends? Can the adolescent voice his/her own opinion?

PHYSICAL DEVELOPMENT

1. Does the adolescent express concern about the onset of puberty? Is there a need for clarification of age norms and process of development? Is there early or late maturation?

2. Are there concerns about the changes which have already occurred (e.g., short stature or acne)?

3. Review nutritional intake and eating habits. Is the adolescent obese? Is there a failure to gain weight?

4. Are there complications in self-image or body image due to medical procedures?

COGNITIVE DEVELOPMENT

1. Are the effects of any medical procedures and/or chronic illness understood?

2. Is there a presence of psychopathology? Is the adolescent overly self-involved, socially withdrawn, and spending much time alone? Is there no reality base to observations? Are there strange associations between ideas, idiosyncratic logic, or overly symbolic thought?

3. Are there self-image issues such as confusion about body size or appearance?

IDENTITY DEVELOPMENT - SOCIALIZATION ISSUES

1. School behavior - After a review of past and present school attendance and performance, are there any inconsistencies and/or symptoms of stress?

2. Career goals and aspirations - Are they realistic? Are they a source of conflict with parents?

3. Peer group assessment and social isolation - How many friends does he/she have? Are there ever long periods of loneliness? Does the adolescent have one place he/she tends to go to meet people?

TABLE 5-3 (cont.)

4. Dating - Is this an issue of conflict for parents? Does the adolescent feel comfortable in such relationships? How sexually active is the person? Is he/she informed about contraception, venereal disease, and pregnancy?

5. In what social activities does the adolescent engage? Do most activities revolve around drugs and/or alcohol?

ASSESSMENT OF DEPRESSION

1. Is the depressive period transitory (episodic)? Is it characterized by mood swings?

2. Do the depressive feelings interfere with everyday functioning? Has eating or sleeping changed? Is there weight loss? Has there been a recent drop in grades, loss of peer contacts, withdrawal from family and social activities?

3. Does the depression relate to a life event? Is there a precipitating cause?

4. Is there a family history of suicide and/or depression?

5. Have there been recent impulsive, frequent accidents?

6. Younger adolescents may show depression by: multiple somatic complaints and/or hypochondriasis; impaired attention and concentration; acting out behaviors; and/or drug usage.

Source: Billingham (1981).

often contribute to these injuries. A very active life-style and poor diet in adolescents may result in infectious mononucleosis. Often this disease goes untreated because of the difficulty in distinguishing illness-induced fatigue from normal fatigue resulting from rapid growth. In addition, adolescents are particularly at risk for venereal disease because they are sexually active and often delay seeking medical attention. Syphilis and gonorrhea have reached epidemic proportions among adolescents. Confidentiality is particularly impor-tant to adolescents seeking medical attention for venereal disease (Wilson 1978). Other complex medical problems that involve adoles-cents and that require special consultation are alcoholism, in increas-ing incidence among young people, and drug abuse.

Adolescent Pregnancy. Each year, one million adolescents become pregnant. Biologically, because their bodies are not yet fully mature, these females are at risk for themselves and their babies. Adolescent pregnancies contribute disproportionately to incidences of low birth weight, prematurity, fetal, neonatal, and infant mortality rates, and complications of pregnancy. Infants born to adolescent girls have a greater chance of being physically handicapped and of having health-related problems later in their lives. Twenty-five percent of these pregnant adolescents get pregnant again within a year after the birth of the first baby, thus multiplying risk factors. Although part of the problem results from lack of information—the majority of girls in one national survey thought ovulation occurred during menstruation (Mussen et al. 1979)—many factors contribute. Lett, Cuskey, and Rudd (in press) found that complexity of regimen contributed to contraceptive compliance problems. The problem of adolescent pregnancy may best be examined by evaluating the effects of specific variables or populations. The conditions that contribute to the pregnancy of a girl who is well informed and who has access to medical care may be different from conditions for a poorer, isolated inner-city adolescent. Recently, Rebesco (1980) articulated the cultural and economic issues that contributed to decisions to become pregnant among inner-city adolescents. She found that for this population becoming pregnant resulted in reductions in the often considerable burdens of family responsibilities and removal from a dangerous school setting to a safe all-girls school. In addition, the primary relationship with the girl's boyfriend and father of the child is maintained and supported by both families, and although the girl's mother may have been initially upset, her attitude often quickly changed. Clearly this and other adolescent health problems are complex and may have long-term ramifications.

Dealing with Death

Suicide is the fourth leading cause of death during adolescence. The number of attempts reaches one-half million per year (Friedman and Sarles 1980). This behavior is complex and has multiple meanings and motivations. The health professional should be aware of depression in the adolescent and make appropriate referrals if a suicide attempt is suspected (see Table 5-3).

Another leading cause of death for this age group is cancer. In such cases, the adolescent is cognitively and emotionally capable of being treated as an adult. Every objective study in the last 10 years has indicated that adolescents with terminal diseases are aware of the seriousness of their predicament, are concerned by any conspiracy of silence, and are anxious to discuss their worries with sympathetic listeners. Discussing the diagnosis with the adolescent does not destroy hope, but rather allows a focus on treatment. This provides emotional strength, even if the likelihood of success might be low. The diagnosis should be revealed in conjunction with an explanation of what can be done and what may be expected, at least in the short term. As with other age groups, the health professional's greatest contributions are in providing knowledge and support while counteracting a natural tendency to withdraw.

SUMMARY

Adolescence is an important stage of transition between childhood and adulthood. Its beginning point, puberty, is a physiological event—like most childhood milestones—but its completion is often defined in psychological and social terms—like the milestones of adult development. The paradox in being not a child and not an adult contributes to the adolescent's often extremely ambivalent feelings and behaviors. Because of this ambivalence, the health professional's role must often be defined for the adolescent and the family. The adolescent may not support medical care unless a confidential, trusting, adult-adult relationship is established. Yet within this relationship the adolescent may be sporadic, unpredictable, self-centered, and inarticulate. Despite these qualities, adolescents are often the most idealistic, enthusiastic, and introspective patients with whom a delightful relationship may be formed.

REFERENCES

Astin, A. W., King, M. R., Light, J. M., and Richardson, G. T. *The American Freshman: National Norms for Fall, 1974.* Los Angeles: University of California Press, 1974.

Bem, S. L. "The measure of psychological androgyny." *Journal of Consulting and Clinical Psychology,* 1974, 42:155–162.

Billingham, K. A. "The behavioral manifestations of fear of success with women and the modifications of such behaviors via a modeling procedure." Doctoral dissertation, DePaul University, Chicago, 1978.

_____. "Behavior Through the Life Cycle: Adolescent Development." Unpublished manuscript, Rush Medical College, Chicago, 1981.

Block, J., and Turula, E. "Identification, ego control, and adjustment." *Child Development,* 1963, 34:945–953.

Blum, R. H. *Horatio Alger's Children.* San Francisco: Jossey-Bass, 1972.

Chinn, P. *Child Health Maintenance.* St. Louis: C. V. Mosby Co., 1974.

Cole, L., and Hall, I. *Psychology of Adolescence.* New York: Holt, Rinehart & Winston, 1970.

Davis, J. A. *Great Aspirations: The Graduate School Plans of American College Seniors.* Chicago: Aldine, 1964.

Diepold, J., and Young, R. D. "Empirical studies of adolescent sexual behavior: A critical review." *Adolescence,* 1979, 14(53):45–64.

Donovan, B. T., and Van der Werfften Bosch, J. "The hypothalamus and sexual maturation in the rat." *Journal of Physiology,* 1959, 147:78–92.

Erikson, E. H. "Autobiographic notes on identity crises." *Daedalus,* 1970, 99 (4):730–759.

_____. *Dimensions of a New Identity.* New York: Norton, 1974.

Flavell, J. H. *Cognitive Development.* Englewood Cliffs, N.J.: Prentice-Hall, 1977.

Freiberg, K. L. *Human Development: A Life Span Approach.* Belmont, Calif.: Wadsworth Publishing, 1979.

Freud, S. *The Ego and the Id.* London: Hogarth, 1950.

Friedenberg, E. Z. *The Vanishing Adolescent.* Boston: Beacon, 1959.

Friedman, S. B., and Sarles, R. M. "'Out of control' behavior in adolescents." *Pediatric Clinics of North America,* 1980, 27(1):97–107.

Froese, A. "Adolescence." *Canada's Mental Health,* 1975, 23(1):9–12.

Gordon, L. B. *Behavioral Intervention in Health Care.* Boulder, Colo.: Westview Press, 1982.

Gross, R. T., and Duke, P. M. "The effect of early versus late physical maturation on adolescent behavior." *Pediatric Clinics of North America,* 1980, 27:71–77.

Hall, G. S. *Adolescence: Its Psychology and its Relationships to Physiology, Anthropology, Sociobiology, Sex, Crime, Religion and Education.* New York: Appleton-Century-Crofts, Vols. 1 and 2, 1904.

Heilbrun, A. B., Jr. "Identification and behavioral ineffectiveness during late adolescence." In E. D. Evans (Ed.), *Adolescents: Readings in Behavior and Development.* New York: Holt, Rinehart & Winston, 1970.

Hofman, A. D. "A rational policy toward consent and confidentiality in adolescent health care." *Journal of Adolescent Health Care,* 1980, 1:9–17.

Horner, M. S. "Toward an understanding of achievement-related conflicts in women." *Journal of Social Issues,* 1972, 28:157–176.

Howe, F., and Ahlum, C. "Women's studies and social change." In A. S. Rossi and A. Calderwood (Eds.), *Academic Women on the Move.* New York: Russell Sage Foundation, 1973.

Illig, R., and Prader, A. "Effect of testosterone and growth hormone secretion in patients with anorchia and delayed puberty." *Journal of Clinical Endocrinology,* 1970, 30:615.

Jessor, S. L., and Jessor, R. "Transition from virginity to nonvirginity among youth: A social-pyschological study over time." *Developmental Psychology,* 1975, 11:473–484.

Kagan, J. "Family experience and the child's development." *American Psychologist,* 1979, 24(10):886–891.

Kimball, A. J., and Campbell, M. M. "Psychologic aspects of adolescent patient health care." *Clinical Pediatrics,* 1979, 18(1):15–25.

Kimmell, D. C. *Adulthood and Aging.* New York: John Wiley and Sons, 1974.

Kogut, M. D. "Growth and development in adolescence." *Pediatric Clinics of North America,* 1973, 20(4):789–806.

Kolodny, R. C., Masters, W. H., and Johnson, V. E. *Textbook of Sexual Medicine.* Boston: Little Brown & Co., 1979.

Lesser, G. S., and Kandel, D. "Parent-adolescent relationships and adolescent independence in the United States and Denmark." *Journal of Marriage and the Family,* 1969, 31:348–358.

Lett, I. F., Cuskey, W. R., and Rudd, S. "Identifying adolescent risk for contraceptive noncompliance." *Journal of Pediatrics* (in press).

Looney, J. G., and Gunderson, E.K.E. "Transient situation disorders: A longitudinal study in young men." *American Journal of Psychiatry,* 1978, 135:660–663.

Looney, J., Oldham, D., and Blotcky, M. "Assessing psychological symptoms in adolescents." *Southern Medical Journal,* 1978, 71(10):1197–1202.

Lowrey, G. H. *Growth and Development of Children.* 7th Ed. Chicago: Year Book Medical Publishers, 1978.

Lynn, D. B. *The Father: His Role in Child Development.* Belmont, Calif.: Wadsworth, 1974.

Marlow, D. R. *Textbook of Pediatric Nursing.* 4th Ed. Philadelphia: W. B. Saunders Co., 1973.

Mathis, J. L. "Adolescent sexuality and societal change." *American Journal of Psychotherapy,* 1976, 30:433–440.

Murray, R. B., and Zentner, J. P. *Nursing Assessment and Health Promotion Through the Life Span.* 2nd Ed. Englewood Cliffs, N.J.: Prentice-Hall, 1979.

Mussen, P. H. *The Psychological Development of the Child.* 2nd Ed. Englewood Cliffs, N.J.: Prentice-Hall, 1973.

Mussen, P. H., Conger, J., and Kagan, J. *Child Development and Personality.* 4th Ed. New York: Harper & Row, 1974.

Mussen, P. H., Conger, J. J., Kagan, J., and Gewitz, J. *Psychological Development: A Life Span Approach.* New York: Harper & Row, 1979.

Muuss, R. E. *Adolescent Behavior and Society.* 2nd Ed. New York: Random House, 1975.

Offer, D. *The Psychological World of the Teenager.* New York: Basic Books, 1969.

Rauh, J. L., Johnson, L. B., and Burket, R. L. "The reproductive adolescent." *Pediatric Clinics of North America,* 1973, 20(4):1005–1019.

Rebesco, M. *Psychological Factors in Adolescent Pregnancy.* Paper presented at the meeting for the Illinois Association of Psychologists in Health and Rehabilitation, February, 1980.

Renshaw, D. C. "Sex and values." *Journal of Clinical Psychiatry,* 1978, 39(9): 716–719.

Shaffer, T. E. "The adolescent athlete." *Pediatric Clinics of North America,* 1973, 20:837–882.

Smith, M. S. "An approach to the adolescent for the primary care clinician." *Journal of Family Practice,* 1979, 8(1):63–66.

Sorenson, R. C. *Adolescent Sexuality in Contemporary America.* New York: World Publishing Co., 1973.

Tanner, J. M. *Growth at Adolescence.* 2nd Ed. Oxford: Blackwell Scientfic Publications, 1962.

Tanner, J. M., Whitehouse, R. H., Hughes, P.C.R., and Vince, F. P. "Effects of human growth hormone treatment for 1 to 7 years on growth of 100 children with growth hormone deficiency, low birth weight, inherited smallness, Turner's Syndrome, and other complaints." *Archives of Diseases in Childhood,* 1971, 46:745.

Tresemer, D. W. *Fear of Success.* New York: Plenum Press, 1977.

Weiner, I., and Del Gaudio, A. "Pschopathology in adolescence." *Archives of General Psychiatry,* 1976, 33:187–193.

Wilkins, L. *The Diagnosis and Treatment of Endocrine Disorders in Childhood and Adolescence.* Springfield, Ill.: Charles C. Thomas, 1965.

Wilson, E. C. "Adolescent moral development and sexual decision in sex and youth: A symposium." *Top of the News.* American Library Association, 1978, 34:145–153.

Wolstenhome, G.E.W., and O'Connor, M. *Endocrinology of the Testis.* Boston: Little, Brown & Co., 1967.

Zelnik, M., and Kantner, J. F. "The resolution of teenage first pregnancies." *Family Planning Perspectives,* 1974, 6(1):74–80.

Zelnick, M., and Kantner, J. F. "Contraceptive patterns and premarital pregnancies among women aged 15–19 in 1976." *Family Planning Perspectives,* 1978, 10:135–142.

INDEX

Freud's theory of, 8
Erikson, Erik H., 10–11
  autonomy vs. shame and doubt,
    77
  identity formation vs. identity
    diffusion, 122–123
  industry vs. inferiority, 98
  initiative vs. guilt, 77
  personality development, 43–44,
    76–77
  play theory, 77–78
  psychosocial crises, 10–11
  trust vs. mistrust, 62–64
Experiments, design of, 12–14
  case history, 13
  cross-sectional method, 13–14
  laboratory setting, 12–13
  longitudinal method, 13–14
  naturalistic setting, 12
  survey, 13
  See also Research, components of

Family, 3
  and adolescence, 109–110,
    125–127
  and early childhood, 60–64
  and infancy development, 20–23
  issues involving parents, 134
  in late childhood, 88–91
  and sex-role identification, 97
  sex-role socialization, 74–75
  siblings, 90–91, 97
  and terminal illness, 81
  See also Father; Mother; Social
    network
Father, 22
  as caretaker, 44
  and divorce, 63–64
  father-son relationship, 90, 97
  late childhood social model,
    88–90
  and pregnancy, 22–23
  as value imparter, 77

See also Family; Mother
Fetus. See Prenatal development
Formal operations. See Piaget,
    cognitive theory of
Freud, Sigmund
  anal stage, 76
  developmental theory of, 8
  ego, 8
  id, 8
  latency, 98
  libido, 7–8
  oral stage, 43
  and personality development, 43
  superego, 8
Friendship. See Peer relationships

Grief, 47, 51–52
  and adoption, 51
  and congenital abnormalities, 51
  and death, 52, 103, 138–139
  See also Death; Terminal illness
Growth, 4
  adolescent, 110–111
  hyperplasia, 4
  hypertrophy, 4
  incremental, 4, 64
  physical, 2, 24
  prenatal influences on, 25–31,
    64–65
  racial patterns of, 111
  replacement, 4
  "secular trend," 112
Growth averages
  adolescent, 110–111
  early childhood, 64–65
  infancy, 35
  late childhood, 91–92
  for newborns, 32–33
  prenatal, 24
  See also Statistical normalcy

Health care
  of adolescents, 132–139